THE
ideals
FAMILY
COOKBOOK
VOL. 2

How sincerely happy we are to present . . . for your enjoyment . . . this volume two of the Ideals Family Cookbook.

As in the first volume, this contains some of your favorite recipes that you've shared with us and with others over the years . . .

The old recipes and the new . . . the everyday and the special occasion ones . . . the treasured and proven successful favorites that have been handed down in your families from generation to generation . . .

And now, presented in keepsake book form, with a little bit of poetry and prose . . . a touch of photography and art . . . we are sure that you will enjoy sharing it with your family and your very special friends.

Maryjane Hooper Tonn
editor

IDEALS PUBLISHING CORP., MILWAUKEE, WIS. 53201
© COPYRIGHT MCMLXXIV, PRINTED AND BOUND IN U.S.A.

Second Printing

CONTENTS

ABBREVIATIONS

t.—teaspoon
T.—tablespoon
c.—cup
pkg.—package
pt.—pint
qt.—quart
oz.—ounce
lb.—pound

FONDUE MEATBALLS

1 lb. ground round or lean hamburger
1 onion, diced
1 t. Accent
½ t. garlic salt
2 t. dried parsley
Salt and pepper to taste

Mix together and shape in balls. Set overnight in refrigerator or freeze.

Cook in fondue pot in hot grease.

Lois Balerud

CHEESE-STUFFED CELERY

1 lb. American cheese
¼ small onion
1 small green bell pepper
1 small can pimientos

Grind all ingredients together. Add salt, pepper, vinegar to taste. Add enough mayonnaise to make a spreading consistency. Spread in celery pieces.

Mrs. Tommy Cochran

3

HOT CRAB DIP

1 7-oz. can crabmeat
10 oz. sharp cheddar cheese
8 oz. sliced American cheese
¼ c. butter
½ c. sauterne wine

Melt all ingredients except crabmeat in a pan. Then add the crabmeat. Serve warm with wheat thin crackers.

Cookie Berning

SAUERKRAUT BALLS

4 T. margarine
1 medium chopped onion
1⅓ c. ground cooked ham
½ minced garlic clove
5 T. flour
3 c. sauerkraut (ground)
1 T. chopped parsley
1 egg
Cracker crumbs

Melt margarine in a large skillet. Sauté onion and add ham and garlic. Cook a few more minutes. Stir in flour and then add ground sauerkraut and parsley. (It should form a stiff paste.) Cool; then form 1-inch balls. Dip in egg to which a little milk has been added. Then roll in cracker crumbs. French fry in deep fat until slightly brown. Put on cookie sheet in warm oven until serving time. The kraut balls can be made a day ahead and then fried when desired.

Mrs. W. Russell McCullough

DEVILED OYSTERS

1 qt. well-drained oysters
2 sticks butter
3 c. bread croutons, mashed
1 small bunch celery
   (cut in small pieces)
¼ c. minced onion
1 T. Worcestershire sauce
1 t. salt
½ t. black pepper

Sauté celery and onion. Add seasoning and mix with croutons and oysters. Place in buttered casserole. Add extra butter for topping and flavor. Bake at 350° until thoroughly heated.

Margaret Welsh

PARTY CHEESE BALL

6 oz. blue cheese
3 jars process cheddar cheese spread
4 oz. cream cheese
2 T. grated onion
1 t. Worcestershire sauce
½ t. Accent
1 c. ground pecans
1 c. chopped parsley

All cheese should be at room temperature. Mix cheese, onion, Worcestershire sauce and Accent together until thoroughly blended. Add ½ c. pecans and ½ c. chopped parsley.

Shape mixture into 1 or 2 balls. Place in bowl lined with waxed paper. Chill overnight.

About 1 hour before serving, roll ball in mixture of remaining pecans and parsley.

Mrs. Robert Brotherton

AVOCADO DIP TIP

3 large ripe avocados (mashed)
¼ c. chopped pimiento (fresh or canned)
¼ c. chopped green onion
¼ c. chopped green chili
1 large ripe tomato (chopped)
   Salt
   Pepper
   Dash of ginger
   Pinch of Italian seasonings
   Pinch of curry powder
   Garlic to taste

Mix together with the avocados (gently, so as not to mush). Chill.

Variations:

Add 1 c. sour cream before serving, or the sour cream may be served with the dip.

Add ½ c. chopped fresh carrots before chilling.

Charles Montgomery

BEEF BURGUNDY STEW

2 lb. beef stew meat
¼ t. marjoram
½ t. dill weed
1 c. Burgundy wine
1½ c. water
2 beef bouillon cubes
2 t. vinegar
½ lb. fresh mushrooms, sliced
1 15-oz. can artichokes, drained and halved
2 8-oz. jars small onions, drained

Cut meat into bite-sized pieces. Add salt, pepper and garlic salt to taste. Roll in flour and brown. Pour off grease. Add marjoram, dill, wine, water, bouillon, vinegar, and onions and simmer until meat is tender, about 2 hours.

Add sliced mushrooms and artichokes and mix gently. Pour into 2-quart casserole. (The meat mixture may be made a day ahead — warm in kettle when adding the mushrooms and artichokes. Then put in casserole.)

Biscuit Ring

1 8-oz. pkg. refrigerator biscuits
¼ c. melted butter or margarine
¼ c. grated parmesan cheese

Separate biscuits. Dip into butter and then into cheese. Arrange around casserole, cheese side up. Bake uncovered in 425° oven 15 to 20 minutes. Makes 8 servings.

Bake an additional package of parmesan biscuits on cookie sheet to serve with dish.

Charlene Myers

MOCK TURTLE SOUP

1 c. potatoes	½ c. carrots
1 c. celery	Salt to taste
⅓ c. onion	

Finely cut above ingredients. Then simmer in a small amount of water until very tender. When done add 2 T. Cheez Whiz, stirring well, and 2 or 3 c. milk and a little water if necessary.

Mrs. William Kremenak

SOUPS AND STEWS

CRAB CHOWDER SUPREME

½ c. chopped onion
½ c. chopped celery
3 T. margarine
3 c. milk
1 can condensed potato soup
1 7½-oz. can flaked crabmeat
1 8-oz. can creamed corn
2 T. chopped pimiento
¼ t. salt
¼ c. dry sherry
¼ c. snipped parsley

In a large saucepan cook onion and celery in butter until tender. Add remaining ingredients except the sherry and parsley. Cook until heated through, stirring often, about 15 minutes. Stir in sherry, add parsley and heat 5 minutes or more. Serves 6.

Janet Avila

Thicken soups with 2 or 3 tablespoons of oatmeal — adds richness and flavor. Barley or rice make good nourishing thickeners, too.

LENTIL FRANKFURTER SOUP

½ lb. lentils
1 pt. water
2 qt. beef stock or ham broth
1 onion, chopped
1 carrot, chopped
½ lb. frankfurters, sliced
Seasonings to taste

Wash lentils and soak overnight in the pint of water in 3-quart saucepan. Do not drain. Add stock and vegetables; bring to a boil and simmer about 2 hours or until lentils are tender. Add frankfurter slices, season to taste; simmer about 10 minutes. (If ham broth is used, bits of ham may be substituted for the frankfurters.)

Edith Pikelny

CHICKEN SOUP DINNER

1 3 to 4-lb. chicken, whole
(fryer or broiler)
5 to 7 carrots
1 each: bunch celery, parsley, parsnip
tied together with white parcel string
1 tomato, peeled
1 kohlrabi, peeled, or 2 small turnips
1 small potato, peeled
2 white onions, whole and peeled
Pinch of Spanish saffron
Salt and pepper
2 chicken bouillon cubes

Put chicken in large pot, cover with cold water, put in above vegetables and spices. When soup comes to a boil, skim foam off the top. Do this about 3 times. This will keep the broth clear. Simmer soup about 1½ hours with cover on pot. Drain the vegetables and chicken into a food strainer, letting clear broth drain into another large pot.

While the soup is simmering start the thin, small egg noodles and drain, ready to use with the clear broth. Do not cook the noodles in broth, as they will cloud the broth. Serve the soup first, making a larger platter of the chicken, turnips, potato and other cooked vegetables.

Cookie Santerre

LAZY-DAY STEW

Arrange 2 lb. raw beef cubes or round steak in a roaster or casserole large enough to hold them in a single layer. Do not brown meat first. Cut potatoes, carrots, onions and celery in large chunks in layer on top of meat. Mix an 8 oz. can tomato sauce with 1 can water and 1 t. sugar. Pour over meat and vegetables. Salt and pepper to taste. Scatter 2 teaspoons quick tapioca on top. Do not stir in. Seal roaster tightly in heavy foil. Place in 325° oven at least 2 hours. Do not open oven during recommended cooking time. When foil is removed, meat will be brown with gravy.

Mrs. W. L. Smith

NEVER-FAIL DUMPLINGS

2 c. flour, sifted
4 t. baking powder
1 t. salt
2 eggs, beaten
½ c. milk
1 T. parsley, finely chopped

Sift flour, baking powder and salt twice. Break eggs into a measuring cup. Add ½ c. milk or more to make 1 cup. Beat eggs and milk thoroughly. Add liquid and parsley to the flour mixture and stir until smooth and stiff. Drop by spoonful over steaming hot soup or stew. Cover. Allow to steam over low heat for 10 minutes. Do not lift the cover. Cooking utensil must always have a tight-fitting cover or dumplings will be heavy.

Virginia Kraegenbrink

FRENCH ONION SOUP

1 can beef consommé
1 large onion
3 slices day-old French bread
3 slices cheese
1 stick butter

Peel and chop onion into small pieces. Heat frying pan and spread with enough butter to sauté onions to taste. Put away extra butter and sauté onions in pan to taste (crisp or light). While onions are being sautéed, put consommé into pot and cook slowly. When onions are done put them in consommé with as much butter from pan as you like. Cook consommé and onions together for 2 minutes. Place soup in individual bowls. Put in each a slice of French bread and cheese. If desired, put bowls in broiler and broil cheese. The cheese will melt naturally. Makes 3 servings.

Deborah Law

LUMBERJACK STEW

2 lb. beef chuck	1 or 2 bay leaves
2 T. fat	1 T. salt
1 T. lemon juice	1 t. pepper
4 c. boiling water	1 t. sugar
1 t. Worcestershire sauce	½ t. paprika
1 clove garlic	6 carrots
1 medium onion, sliced	1 lb. small onions (optional)

Cut meat in 1½-inch cubes. Thoroughly brown on all sides in hot fat; add water, lemon juice, Worcestershire sauce, garlic, sliced onion, bay leaves and seasonings.

Cover and simmer 2 hours, stirring occasionally. Add carrots (and onions if desired). Cover and cook 30 minutes or more, until vegetables are tender. Thicken liquid for gravy if desired.

Carole A. Davis

SALADS

CHRISTMAS SALAD

1 pkg. lemon gelatin
2 c. hot cranberry juice cocktail
1 banana
1 T. lemon juice
½ c. crushed pineapple
½ c. finely chopped celery

Dissolve gelatin in cranberry juice which has been slightly sweetened and chill. Slice banana and cover with lemon juice. Add pineapple and chopped celery to banana and fold all into slightly thickened gelatin. Turn into individual molds. Chill until firm. Unmold on crisp lettuce. Serve with cranberry mayonnaise made by folding ½ c. heavy cream whipped into ⅓ c. mayonnaise. Add a sprinkling of salt and 1½ T. cranberry juice cocktail. If a sweeter dressing is desired, add a small amount of confectioners' sugar.

Lilian B. Morse

PINEAPPLE-APRICOT SALAD

2 pkgs. orange gelatin
2 c. hot water
½ c. pineapple juice
½ c. apricot juice
1 #2½ can pineapple tidbits
1 #2½ can apricots, cut up
¾ c. miniature white marshmallows

Dissolve gelatin in hot water. Add pineapple and apricot juices (instead of cold water). Chill until partially congealed. Add pineapple, apricots and marshmallows; chill until firm and add topping.

Topping

¼ c. sugar
½ c. pineapple juice
½ c. apricot juice
3 T. flour
2 T. butter
1 egg
1 c. whipping cream, whipped

Combine first 6 ingredients in saucepan; bring to a boil. Let cool; then fold in whipped cream. Place topping on gelatin, then sprinkle with grated cheddar cheese.

Mrs. Gaillard A. Parrish

BACON-CAULIFLOWER SALAD

Prepare the following recipe the night before in a large bowl that can be tightly covered.

1 head lettuce   1 lb. bacon
1 onion   ½ head cauliflower

Break up lettuce and cauliflower in pieces. Section onion into rings. Fry bacon and cut up. Layer in order listed above. Sprinkle over the top the following ingredients:

¼ c. sugar
1 c. mayonnaise or salad dressing
⅓ c. parmesan cheese
    Salt and pepper to taste

Cover tightly until ready to serve. Mix well before serving.

Beryl Sink

SALAD TIPS

For a subtle garlic flavor, rub the salad bowl with a cut clove of garlic. For a more pronounced flavor, mince the garlic very fine and crush it with a little salt. Add to the salad.

Use a variety of greens. In addition to the popular Iceberg lettuce, try Bibb and Boston lettuce; or tender young spinach leaves, dandelion greens, escarole and romaine.

Accent your salad bowl of greens with a variety of cooked vegetables or boiled eggs and a sprinkling of herbs. Herbs with an affinity for salads are basil, marjoram, thyme, tarragon and parsley.

Make your salad bowl attractive, add eye appeal with garnishes of color — red and green sweet pepper rings, sliced stuffed olives, whole pitted ripe olives. Or try a sprinkling of cheese cubes on top, or even fruit bits added as trimming, such as a few pineapple cubes, a border of mandarin orange sections around the bowl and a cherry in center. Even vegetable salads may wear a crown of fruit for extra flavor.

Strips of crisp bacon, crumbled, provide flavor contrast to many salads.

Johnielu Barber Bradford

CAESAR SALAD

4 c. torn lettuce
4 slices bacon, crumbled
¾ c. croutons
6 small tomatoes, halved
3 sprigs watercress
3 T. olive oil
1½ T. lemon juice
1 egg
2 T. Caesar salad mix

Add bacon and croutons to lettuce. Add salad mix, tomatoes and watercress. Combine olive oil and lemon juice. Pour over salad. Break egg on top, mix well.

Caesar Salad Mix

1½ t. garlic salt
½ t. dry mustard
½ t. oregano
½ t. pepper
1 c. parmesan cheese

Mix all ingredients in a jar and store in refrigerator.

Jane F. Prudden

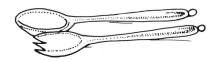

SEAFOOD SALAD

2 qt. water
1½ T. salt
6 oz. seashell macaroni
1 c. cut celery
1 c. cooked peas
1 4½-oz. can small shrimp, rinsed and drained
1 4½-oz. can sliced water chestnuts
1 T. cut chives

Bring water to a boil. Add salt and macaroni and cook until tender. Keep firm to hold shape. Drain and rinse in cold water. Add remaining ingredients. Then blend 2 T. vinegar, 1 t. mustard, 2 T. sugar, ¼ t. salt and ¼ c. half and half (milk and cream). Mix with 1 c. salad dressing. Serve in wide bowl lined with greens. Garnish with 1 can shrimp prepared as above and 3 hard-boiled eggs, quartered.

Minnie Klemme

COOKED SALAD DRESSING

2 c. sugar
3 T. prepared mustard
1¼ t. salt
3 T. flour
3 eggs
¼ c. milk
1½ T. butter
¾ c. sour cream
½ c. vinegar

Combine all ingredients except butter in the following order: sugar, salt, mustard, flour, eggs, sour cream, milk and vinegar. Blend thoroughly. Cook over hot water, stirring constantly, until thickened. Add butter, blend thoroughly. Salad dressing keeps well if refrigerated.

Mrs. Paul Burkhart

MIX-AND-FIX-AHEAD PEA SALAD

1 can tiny peas
1 c. diced soft cheese
1 c. chopped peanuts
¼ c. chopped pimiento
6 sweet pickles, chopped

Toss together and mix with mayonnaise. Serve well chilled on lettuce leaves.

Lois J. Martinec

HOT CHICKEN SALAD

4 c. stewed chicken breasts, cubed
1 heaping c. celery, sliced diagonally
1 can water chestnuts, sliced
1 c. cooked rice
1 heaping c. cooked frozen peas
½ t. salt
¼ t. garlic salt
2 c. mayonnaise
6 T. lemon juice (can use frozen juice)
4 T. minced dried onions
2 t. Worcestershire sauce
2 t. prepared mustard

Combine the above ingredients, toss lightly, put in a casserole. Top with grated cheese and 3 or 4 slices of fried crisp bacon, crumbled. Lastly, add corn-chip crumbs or any favorite crumbs. Bake in 450° oven for 10 minutes. Makes 8 servings.

Helen L. King

SANDWICHES

PIMIENTO-BEEF SANDWICH SPREAD

2 c. freshly cooked soupbone beef
1/3 c. mayonnaise
1 hard-boiled egg
1/2 c. pimiento, finely cut
1/8 t. salt

Shred meat. Mash egg to a smooth consistency with small amount of mayonnaise. Add salt with pimiento, stirring into meat. Mix in remainder of the mayonnaise, and spread on slices of white bread. Top with whole wheat bread, cut into finger sandwiches, and place on plate with part brown and part white bread showing.

Virginia K. Oliver

CHIPPED HAM SANDWICH

2 lb. chipped spiced ham, broken in small pieces
1/2 lb. sharp cheese, grated
3 hard-cooked eggs, grated
1 12-oz. bottle chili sauce
1/2 c. salad dressing

Mix all ingredients together. Spread on weiner buns. Wrap in aluminum foil. Heat in 350° oven about 15 minutes. May be frozen. Makes approximately 36 sandwiches.

Mrs. Paul J. Clark

PIZZA BURGERS

1 lb. ground beef
1/2 lb. pork sausage
1 c. shredded mozzarella cheese
1 medium-size can or jar spaghetti sauce
1 t. sage
1 t. oregano
1 T. parsley flakes
12 hamburger buns

Crumble and brown ground beef and pork sausage. Drain fat and cool. Add sage, oregano, parsley flakes, spaghetti sauce and cheese. Portion onto halved buns. Place on cookie sheet. Bake 10 to 12 minutes at 425°. Makes 24 pizza burgers.

Gail A. Hirdler

SURPRISE SANDWICH

1 lb. ring of baloney
3/4 lb. sharp American cheese
1/4 c. mustard
1/3 c. salad dressing
1 t. minced onions
2 T. chopped sweet pickle or relish

Grind baloney, grate cheese. Add rest of ingredients. Mix well. Use weiner or hamburger buns. Wrap in foil. Heat in 325° oven for 25 minutes. Makes about 16 or 18 sandwiches.

Mrs. E. Stillman Gates

RECIPE FOR PIONEER MOTHERS

One large portion of hospitality,
Add the same amount of charity,
Add one part fairness,
One part self-sacrifice,
One part honesty,
One part tolerance,
One part understanding,
One part wisdom,
One part kindness,
One part gentleness,
And one part humility.
Season with perfect faith in God.

Mix all ingredients together and completely submerge in love. Now you have the perfect recipe for our pioneer mothers.

Clara Edgbert Schlottmann

OPEN-FACE SANDWICHES

1/2 c. grated American process cheese
3 eggs, finely chopped
1/4 c. finely chopped green pepper
1 1/2 t. grated onion
1/3 c. canned milk
3 T. catsup
1/4 t. salt

Mix together and place on hamburger buns. Bake 7 minutes at 400°.

Mrs. Kenneth E. Coon

POINSETTIA SANDWICH "CAKE"

Trim all crust off top and bottom of 1 round white loaf of bread. Slice loaf in 3 circles 1 inch in width. Spread each circle with soft butter. Spread bottom slice with ham filling; top with slice of bread and cover with egg filling. Top with third slice, with buttered side next to egg filling. Chill several hours wrapped in clear plastic wrap.

Ham Filling

2 4½-oz. cans or 2 c. chopped cooked ham
⅓ c. pickle relish
¼ c. chopped celery

Mix well.

Egg Filling

5 hard-cooked eggs, well chopped
⅓ c. chopped stuffed olives
⅓ c. mayonnaise
1½ t. prepared mustard
1 t. grated onion
Salt and pepper to taste

Mix well.

Trimming

16 oz. cream cheese
⅓ c. light cream

Beat until smooth and fluffy. Spread on sides and top of loaf. Trim top with a poinsettia cut from pimiento. Use sifted hard-cooked egg yolks for center of poinsettia. Decorate sides with holly leaves cut from green peppers. Serves 10.

Mrs. Leland Kitzenberg

11

 # RELISHES

THE CUCUMBER CRAZE

The cucumber craze starts in summertime
And lasts all year long
In pickles, relishes, and spreads
That ease the winter along.

Please try this recipe of mine
To aid the salad scene;
It takes three cukes sliced very thin
And a cup of sour cream.

Add onions, diced, a half a cup,
And mix together well;
Add salt to taste and pepper too,
And you've a treat that's swell.

When cucumbers come, they come on
strong,
And you are sure to find
That eating them as they may grow
Will leave you far behind.

So plan ahead for wintertime
With this quick recipe
Which gives you dills without a crock
As simply as can be.

Just wash your cukes until they're clean,
And sterilize quart jars;
Then fill with cukes, two sprigs of dill,
And all is well so far.

You need to make a pickling brine
Of vinegar one cup,
With water in the same amount
And let it boil up.

When it has boiled five minutes long,
Add to the filled quart jars,
And seal them yet while very hot,
And finished now you are.

Craig E. Sathoff

KRAUT RELISH

1 lb. can sauerkraut
3 c. finely sliced celery
2 c. finely sliced onion
1 c. finely sliced green pepper
½ c. mild vinegar
1 c. granulated sugar

Mix all ingredients and allow to stand, refrigerated, one to three days.

Mrs. Ervin Foor, Sr.

PICKLED SWEET PEPPERS

1 peck red and green sweet peppers
1 large onion
2½ c. sugar
1½ qt. cider vinegar
3½ qt. water
1½ c. corn oil
½ c. salt
1 T. celery seed
1 T. mustard seed
1 T. dill seed
1 clove garlic

Wash and core raw peppers; cut in two and push into clean, sterilized jars. Makes about 10 jars.

Mix all other ingredients together, leave onion and clove of garlic whole and drop into mixture. Heat to boiling. Dip or pour over peppers. Run a knife down the sides of jars to let out air bubbles. Seal at once with regular canning caps and rings. You can add onion and clove of garlic to last jar if desired.

Ruby Davenport Kish

CORN RELISH

12 ears white corn
4 stalks celery
2 onions
6 peppers (sweet red and green)
1 t. celery seed
2 T. powdered mustard
2 T. salt
3 c. granulated sugar
1 qt. sweet cider vinegar

Boil 20 minutes. Put in pint jars. Yields 6 pints.

Mrs. Lester C. Place

GRANDMA'S BEET PICKLES

1 pt. strong vinegar
1 pt. sugar
6 pt. water
1 T. salt
8½ qt. cooked, sliced or quartered beets

Heat beets in hot solution. Pack in sterilized jars and seal.

Leietta M. Taylor

CREAMED CUCUMBERS

2 large cucumbers, pared and sliced thin
1½ t. salt

Mix above together well and let stand. In the meantime, mix together the following:

1 c. dairy sour cream
2 T. lemon juice
1 T. finely chopped onion
1 t. sugar
    Dash of pepper

Drain cucumbers, top with sour cream dressing and refrigerate, about 2 hours. Sprinkle 1½ t. chopped parsley over the dish when ready to serve.

Mabel White Epling

FESTIVE BAKED EGGPLANT

1 large eggplant
½ medium onion, chopped
3 T. butter or margarine
3 T. chopped parsley
1 can cream of mushroom soup
    Worcestershire sauce to taste
    Salt and pepper to taste
    24 round buttery crackers, crumbled
    Cheese strips
    Pimiento to garnish

Cut off eggplant top, scrape out inside, leaving a quarter of the shell intact. Parboil the eggplant meat in a little salt water until tender. Drain thoroughly.

Sauté onion in butter, stir in parsley, add to the cooked eggplant. Add soup and seasonings. Add crumbled crackers and pile mixture into eggplant shell. Bake at 375° for 25 to 30 minutes. Remove from oven and add cheese strips or grated cheese and return to oven and bake about 10 minutes longer or until cheese is melted.

Before serving, dot the top with pea-size bits of chopped pimiento or sliced stuffed olive for added color. Serves 4.

Johnielu Barber Bradford

"DRESSED-UP" GREEN BEANS

1 medium onion, chopped
½ green pepper, chopped
¼ c. cooking oil
½ c. catsup
1 t. sugar
    Salt and pepper

Simmer above ingredients for 20 minutes, then add canned string beans. Simmer again ½ hour.

Caroline Taber

Cauliflower keeps white if you put a tablespoon of lemon juice or white vinegar in the cooking water.

Vegetable odors vanish if you place an open dish of vinegar on the stove or nearby counter while cooking.

Keep vegetables fresh and rust-free by wrapping them in paper toweling when you store them.

NEVER-FAIL RICE

1 medium onion, minced
2 T. butter
1 c. long grain, raw white rice
2 c. hot chicken broth

Sauté onion in the butter until transparent. Add rice and hot broth. Bring *to* a boil (uncovered), but do not boil. Cover and place in a 325° oven for 20 minutes.

Mrs. George Nordmann

SPINACH SOUFFLÉ

⅓ c. onion, finely chopped	3 T. butter
2 T. flour	3 egg yolks
1 c. light cream	1 c. cooked, cut spinach
3 egg whites	⅓ c. diced cheese
¼ t. salt	⅛ t. pepper

Melt 1 T. butter in a saucepan, add onion and brown. Blend flour smoothly into cream, add 2 T. butter with salt and pepper. Pour over onions and stir slowly as mixture thickens. Whip egg yolks until thick. Add spinach with cheese and blend into sauce. Beat egg whites until they form stiff peaks, then stir into mixture. Pour into greased casserole. Place in pan of water heated to boiling point, and bake in 350° oven 1 hour.

Virginia K. Oliver

SPECIAL GIFT SURPRISES

Jellies, pink and purple,
    From the kitchen of a friend;
Homemade rolls and cookies
    Or a special candy blend.
From the neighbor's garden come
    Green onions, fresh snap beans,
Bright orange carrots crisp,
    Just-picked peas, Swiss chard greens.

Green corn, fresh off the stalk,
    Vine-ripened red tomatoes,
Dark, wine-red beets just dug,
    And early new potatoes.
Fresh cherries for the picking
    From the next-door neighbor's tree;
Just for gathering from the ground,
    Dropped pears and apples, free.

When one has had a garden
    And a background on the farm,
These gifts have special meaning
    With a certain kind of charm.
Besides the time and labor,
    Behind this kind of gift,
Are the thoughtfulness and love
    That give us such a lift.

Agnes Drake

FRIED TOMATOES

6 large beefsteak tomatoes
Salt and pepper
Garlic salt
Fine, dry crumbs
2 T. each butter and bacon fat
1 T. flour
½ t. basil
½ t. paprika
1½ c. sour cream
Chopped green onions

Cut tomatoes (half ripe, if possible) in ¾-inch slices. Add salt, pepper, and garlic salt and coat with crumbs. Melt half of the butter and bacon fat in a large skillet and let it get very hot. Sauté tomatoes quickly on both sides, turning carefully. Remove, add more fat to skillet if needed. Add 1 t. salt and next 3 ingredients, stirring. Add sour cream slowly over low heat. Heat just to thicken. Pour over tomatoes and top with green onions. Serves 6.

Estella Long Black

WILTED LETTUCE

6 slices bacon	1 onion, diced
⅓ c. vinegar	Salt and pepper
2 T. sugar	

Cut bacon into small pieces, fry crisp. Heat ingredients to boiling, pour over shredded lettuce. Mix well.

Mrs. Charles Peters

SCALLOPED ASPARAGUS

2 cans cut asparagus spears (or 2½ c. cooked fresh asparagus)
3 c. medium white sauce
1 c. buttered bread crumbs
5 hard-boiled eggs, sliced
4 T. chopped pimiento
Salt and pepper to taste

Arrange asparagus, egg slices, and pimiento in a 2-quart greased casserole. Cover with white sauce, then top with bread crumbs. Bake at 375° about 25 minutes or until golden brown.

Mrs. Coy Wilcoxson

POTATOES ALASKA

2 c. mashed potatoes
2 T. butter or margarine
2 egg yolks
2 T. chopped green onion tops
½ t. salt
2 egg whites
2 T. salad dressing
½ t. lemon juice
Dash of pepper

Add butter, egg yolks, onion tops, salt and pepper to mashed potatoes (potatoes should not have milk or seasoning added beforehand). Mix well. Spoon 6 mounds onto a foil-covered baking sheet.

Beat egg whites to stiff peaks, folding in salad dressing and lemon juice. Top each potato mound with egg white mixture. Bake in 350° oven 10 to 12 minutes, or until egg whites are golden. Serves 6.

Mrs. E. Moore

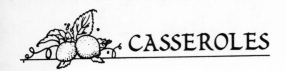

CASSEROLES

SHRIMP CASSEROLE

16 slices cheddar cheese
2 lb. cleaned, cooked shrimp
2 large cans evaporated milk
2 eggs

Melt cheddar cheese in double boiler. When melted, add evaporated milk and eggs. Beat lightly with egg beater to eliminate any lumps. Place in casserole, add shrimp, and sprinkle generously with bread crumbs. Bake about 1 hour at 350°. Serve on toast points, in flaky patty shells or plain.

Bonnie Shorey

RICE AND MUSHROOM DISH

1 c. rice, uncooked
1 stick margarine
  Onion salt
  Garlic salt
  Paprika
1 can beef consommé
½ c. water
1 small can mushrooms (pieces and
  stems), well drained

Sauté rice in margarine until light golden brown; sprinkle generously with salts and paprika. Combine with consommé and water. Bake uncovered at 350° for 45 minutes. Remove from oven, top with mushrooms and bake 15 minutes longer. Serves 6.

Mrs. Ralph Frazier

CORNED BEEF CASSEROLE

2 c. cooked macaroni
1 12-oz. can corned beef
¼ lb. processed cheese, cubed
1 10-oz. can cream of chicken soup
1 c. milk
½ c. chopped onions
¾ c. buttered crumbs

Combine ingredients, mix well. Top with crumbs. Bake at 375° for 60 minutes.

Pollyanna Sedziol

QUICK-AS-A-WINK HOT DISH

  Sliced raw potatoes
1½ lb. hamburger
2 cans vegetable beef soup (undiluted)

Place the potatoes in the bottom of a baking dish. Crumble hamburger and place over potatoes. Add vegetable beef soup. Cover with foil and bake for 1½ hours. Remove foil last ½ hour of baking time.

Mrs. Manford Dale

EASY CHILI CASSEROLE

1 lb. hamburger
1 large onion, chopped fine

Brown lightly in a small amount of butter.

1¼ t. salt
1¼ t. chili powder
1 small can tomato soup

Drain liquid from 1 can of red kidney beans. Add to the above. Put into a casserole dish and bake at 350° for about 1 hour.

Mrs. A. B. Babcock

TUNA-ASPARAGUS CASSEROLE

3 oz. potato chips
7 oz. can tuna fish
10 oz. can cream of mushroom soup
1 can asparagus, drained

Pat potato chips lightly until broken. Then put into a large mixing bowl. Flake tuna fish and add to the potato chips. Add soup to the above and mix well.

Grease casserole dish. In bottom of dish place the asparagus spears. Then pour the tuna mixture over the asparagus and top with grated cheese. Bake in 350° oven for 30 minutes (or less if in shallow baking dish).

Mr. & Mrs. Richard Davis

HAMBURGER STROGANOFF

¼ c. butter
½ c. minced onion
1 lb. lean ground beef
1 clove garlic (split in half)
2 T. flour
2 t. salt
½ t. pepper
½ lb. fresh mushrooms, sliced
1 can cream of chicken soup
1 c. sour cream

Melt butter in a heavy skillet. Add onion and cook slowly until soft. Add ground beef and garlic; stir until browned. Stir in flour, salt, pepper and mushrooms. Cook 5 minutes. Add soup; simmer 10 minutes or longer. Just before serving, remove garlic, stir in sour cream and heat through. Serve over rice or noodles. Serves 6 to 8.

Arlene Clark

Rice grains stay white and separated if you add a teaspoon of lemon juice to each quart of cooking water.

GERMAN MEAT CASSEROLE

3 large potatoes, sliced thin
5 carrots, quartered
1 small onion, diced
2 T. butter
2 lbs. ground meat
1 T. catsup
1 10½-oz. can cream of mushroom soup
1 4-oz. can button mushrooms, drained
1 3½-oz. can French fried onion rings

Parboil potatoes and carrots for 20 minutes. Sauté onion in 2 T. butter, add beef and cook until it turns gray. Butter a 2½-quart casserole dish. Alternate layers of beef-onion mixture and vegetables. Mix catsup with soup and pour over casserole. Sauté mushrooms in 3 T. butter and place on top of casserole. Sprinkle onion rings over mushrooms. Bake at 350° about 20 minutes or until onion rings are brown and crisp. Yield: 6 servings.

Helen Foreman

HALE-AND-HEARTY CASSEROLE

1 8-oz. pkg. wide noodles
1 pkg. frozen peas
1 can cream of chicken or cream of mushroom soup
1 c. diced chicken
1 small finely minced onion
1 strip red or green pepper (optional)

Boil noodles for about 12 minutes in salted water. Gently boil peas for about 5 minutes (separately). Drain noodles and peas and place in 1½-quart buttered casserole. Add diced meat, onion and undiluted soup. Add finely cut pepper. Mix well and place ½ c. buttered bread crumbs on top. Bake at 350° for about 25 minutes.

Mrs. Paul W. Fatzinger

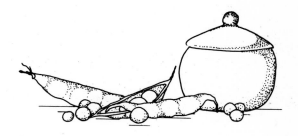

SQUASH CASSEROLE

4 c. diced yellow squash
  Pepper to taste
2 T. grated onion
⅓ c. grated carrots
1 can cream of chicken soup
1 c. sour cream
2 c. prepared package stuffing
3 T. butter
  Slivered almonds (optional)

Cook squash in 1½ c. water to which ¾ t. salt has been added for about 10 minutes. Drain and add next 5 ingredients. Butter a baking dish and put 1 c. stuffing in the bottom. Add squash mixture, top with remaining stuffing and dot with butter. Also sprinkle with almonds if desired. Bake at 350° for 30 minutes.

Mary Cunnyngham

BACON AND BEAN CASSEROLE

2 large cans red kidney beans
2 T. bacon fat
1 clove garlic, minced
1 pinch thyme
1 pinch rosemary
1 small bay leaf, crumbled
6 whole cloves
1 t. salt
2 t. dry mustard
¼ t. cayenne pepper
2 T. strong cider vinegar
½ c. juice from pickled peaches or pears
  (or canned fruit that is not too sweet)
8 slices Canadian bacon cut ¼-inch thick
1 large onion sliced in rings
¼ c. strong black coffee
1 jigger brandy (optional)

Drain beans lightly. Mix together melted bacon fat, all spices, vinegar and juice in a heat-proof casserole. Pour in beans and stir to distribute spices and liquid. Place onion rings on top, then slices of Canadian bacon. Cover with foil or lid, and bake at 300° for 1 hour. Remove cover, pour coffee over meat and bake 15 more minutes at 350°. Shut off oven, and pour brandy over all. Leave about 5 minutes, then serve.

Mrs. H. P. Nielsen

NORTH DAKOTA CASSEROLE

1½ lb. veal
1½ c. chopped onions and celery
1 c. diced green peppers

Cut veal in ½-inch cubes, and fry in fat. Cook until tender but not brown. Add ½ c. rice and 1 can condensed mushroom soup, 1 c. water, 1 can peas (drained), 3 T. chopped pimiento, 1 T. soy sauce, salt and pepper. Bake 1½ hours in a 9 x 13-inch baking dish. Top with 1 can chow mein noodles. Bake 5 more minutes. Add juice of peas if too dry.

Lois Balerud

SEMOLINA SPECIAL

4 T. butter
2 T. flour
2 c. milk
¾ c. shredded cheese
1 can chopped pimientos
3 hard-boiled eggs, sliced
¼ c. chopped green peppers
2 c. macaroni, cooked
½ c. stuffed olives, coarsely cut
1 small can mushrooms (optional)
  Salt and pepper to taste

Make a white sauce of the first 3 ingredients. Add cheese and melt. Add remaining ingredients and mix together. Place in greased casserole and bake at 375° for about 25 minutes or until bubbly.

Leona A. Howell

SWISS CHEESE CASSEROLE

Cook two 9-oz. pkgs. frozen French-style green beans until tender. Drain well. In a saucepan put:

2 T. (heaping) flour
2 T. butter
1 t. salt
2 t. sugar
3 or 4 t. finely grated onion

Make a paste of above ingredients and remove from heat. Add 1 pt. sour cream and 8 oz. grated Swiss cheese. Mix well. Mix beans with the sauce and put in greased casserole.

Put 1 c. cornflake crumbs and 2 T. butter in pan. Heat until butter melts. Place on top of casserole. Bake at 350° for 20 to 25 minutes. Serves 6 to 8.

Norma McKenzie

HAWAIIAN SAUSAGE CASSEROLE

- 1 20-oz. can pineapple chunks in pineapple juice
- 1 18-oz. can sweet potatoes sliced 1-inch thick
- 1 12-oz. pkg. smoked link sausage sliced at 1-inch intervals
- 3 T. brown sugar
- 2 T. cornstarch
- ¼ t. salt
- 1 T. margarine

Drain pineapple. Reserve ¼ c. juice in measuring cup and add water to make 1 cup.

Arrange potatoes, pineapple chunks and sausage in a buttered 10 x 6 x 1¾-inch baking dish. Four of the cut sausage links can be placed between the potatoes and pineapple chunks and the balance of the four cut links placed on top.

In a small saucepan combine brown sugar, cornstarch and salt. Gradually blend in the pineapple juice with water. Cook and stir until thickened and bubbly. Cook and stir 1 minute, remove from heat, stir in margarine.

Pour over potatoes, pineapple and sausage mixture in casserole. Cover and bake at 350° for 40 minutes to 1 hour or until bubbly. Makes 4 servings.

Mrs. Werner Kreimeier

BROCCOLI AND ONION CASSEROLE

- 2 pkg. frozen broccoli
- 1 small can white onions, drained

Cook frozen broccoli in boiling water for a few minutes. Arrange in an 8 x 10-inch baking dish, heads to sides and stems toward center. Slit the stems. Spread the onions over this and pour over all the cheddar cheese sauce which has been made ahead of time.

Make this sauce with milk and 1 T. flour. After it thickens add grated cheese. Stir for a few minutes and spread over the broccoli and onions in the baking dish. Bake in 325° oven for about 30 minutes. Serves 6.

Edith Goodrich Cox

CHICKEN

BARBECUED CHICKEN

Roll 1 cut-up frying chicken in flour and brown in ¼ c. oil.

½ c. catsup
⅓ c. water
2 T. lemon juice
1 T. each: brown sugar, vinegar, prepared mustard, Worcestershire sauce
Garlic salt to taste
Onion salt to taste

Bring above ingredients to a boil and pour over chicken that has been arranged in casserole. Cover and bake in 350° oven for 1¼ hours.

Bertha V. Huber

GREEN NOODLE CHICKEN

1 3-lb. fryer
1 c. chopped celery
1 medium onion
1 medium green pepper
1 can mushroom soup
12 oz. American cheese
5 oz. green noodles
1 stick margarine
3 oz. bottle stuffed olives, chopped

Boil, bone and chop chicken. Cook noodles in chicken stock, letting noodles stand to soak up as much broth as possible. Cook celery, onion and pepper in margarine until soft. Add cheese to the warm celery, onion and pepper to melt. Combine all ingredients in a casserole. Bake at 325° until heated thoroughly.

Howell Intermediate School

CHICKEN SQUARES

2 c. diced, cooked chicken
1 c. broken, cooked spaghetti
1 c. grated cheese
1½ c. chicken broth
3 eggs, beaten
¼ c. melted butter

Mix above ingredients together and bake at 300° for 1 hour in an 8 x 8-inch square pan. Serve with a can of undiluted mushroom soup poured over the top. Makes 6 servings.

Nancy Watts

THE DIFFERENCE

There is a difference between dining and eating.

Dining is an art.

When you eat to get the most out of your meal and to please the palate, just as well as to satiate the appetite.

That, my friend, is dining.

Yuan Mia
1739 A.D.

FILE GUMBO

Boil 1 chicken until tender. In a separate skillet, make a medium roux by browning flour in bacon drippings and stirring until golden brown. Before completely browned, add 2 T. finely chopped onion and finish browning, being careful not to let it burn. Add water to make a gravy.

Add this gravy to the boiled chicken, cut into serving pieces, and part of the broth from chicken. Add more broth if needed to make a soup consistency. Add salt and pepper to taste. Simmer 15 to 20 minutes over low heat. Just before serving, add 1 heaping teaspoon filé. Serve over cooked rice.

Note: Filé is powdered leaves of sassafras which cook dark green and thick. It is used in Creole cookery, especially gumbos.

Ann Donovan

SWEET-AND-SOUR CHICKEN

2½ lb. chicken
⅓ c. shortening
⅓ c. vinegar
½ c. firmly packed dark-brown sugar
1 12-oz. can unsweetened pineapple
    juice
¾ c. catsup
⅛ t. salt
1 T. soy sauce
1 t. prepared mustard

Brown unbreaded chicken, remove from skillet. Drain drippings from skillet and add vinegar, sugar, juice, catsup, soy sauce, mustard and salt to skillet. Bring to a boil, stirring occasionally. Boil 5 minutes. Add browned chicken; simmer, covered, 20 minutes. Turn chicken and cook uncovered 20 minutes longer or until tender. Remove chicken to serving dish. Skim fat from sauce, if necessary. Pour sauce over chicken.

Mrs. Jacob Baldinger

GOOD-LUCK STUFFING

1½ c. rice
4 T. butter
½ c. chopped celery
½ c. chopped onions
½ c. chopped green pepper
½ c. chopped walnuts
½ c. chopped apples
½ c. chopped green olives
1 t. soy sauce
½ T. sugar
1 t. salt
½ t. pepper
    Dash monosodium glutamate

Cook rice, melt butter, add raw food, fry; add rice and fry gently. Add seasoning. Stuff bird lightly.

George A. McDonald

KING RANCH CHICKEN

2 pkg. (12 to each pkg.) tortillas
1 large fryer or hen
1 large onion, chopped
1 large bell pepper, chopped
½ lb. grated cheddar cheese
1 T. chili powder
    Garlic to taste
2 cans cream of chicken soup
1 can cream of mushroom soup
1 can tomatoes with chilies, crushed

Boil and bone the chicken. Cut into bite-sized pieces. Dip each tortilla in boiling chicken stock to soften. Place the ingredients in layers in a 9 x 12-inch baking dish in order listed. Bake at 350° for 30 minutes. Serves 6 to 8.

Mrs. Rayburn Buice

CHICKEN DELIGHT

1 frying chicken
1 c. uncooked rice
1½ c. milk
1 t. salt
1 can cream of mushroom soup
1 can cream of chicken soup
½ c. milk

Cover bottom of a greased 2-quart baking dish with the uncooked rice, pour 1½ c. milk over rice and add the salt. Spread cut-up chicken on top of rice. Combine the soups and ½ c. milk and pour over the chicken. Bake 2 hours at 250° or until done.

Susan Robinson

Don't crowd your oven. Place pans no less than an inch from the oven walls. Heat must circulate freely for best results. Stagger pans, too — don't place one directly over the other.

No fry pan explosions if you sprinkle a little salt in the pan first before starting to fry food.

MEAT

SPICED-APPLE BEEF PATTIES

1 lb. ground beef
1 c. cooked rice
1 egg, slightly beaten
1 t. salt
1 t. Worcestershire sauce
5 spiced apple rings (half of 5-oz. jar)
¼ c. corn syrup
1 T. lemon juice
2 t. cornstarch

Combine thoroughly meat, rice, ½ c. water, the egg, salt and Worcestershire sauce. Shape into 5 thick patties. Place in shallow baking pan. Drain apple rings, saving ½ c. syrup. Press an apple ring onto each patty. Bake uncovered in a 350° oven for 35 minutes. Meanwhile, combine saved apple syrup and lemon juice in a saucepan. Stir 2 t. water into the cornstarch. Add to syrup mixture. Cook and stir until mixture is thickened and bubbly. Spoon onto patties. Bake 5 more minutes. Makes 5 servings.

Florence Howard

MOCK CHICKEN WITH DUMPLINGS

1 lb. veal
2 stalks celery, chopped
1 medium onion, diced
½ t. salt
¼ t. pepper
1 can condensed chicken soup
2 c. all-purpose flour
4 t. baking powder
¼ t. salt
3 level T. shortening
⅔ c. milk

Cut veal into small pieces. Add first 4 ingredients. Cover with water and cook until veal is tender. Add 1 can condensed chicken soup and bring to a rolling boil. Add dumplings made by sifting flour with baking powder and salt. Blend in shortening. Moisten with milk and drop by spoonsful into boiling broth. Cover and let simmer 15 minutes without uncovering.

Joy Belle Burgess

SOUTHERN-STYLE STEAK WITH NOODLES

1½ c. noodles
1 lb. ground steak
1 T. butter
1⅓ c. tomato juice
½ t. salt
⅓ c. cut celery
⅓ c. minced onion
¾ c. chopped green pepper
¾ c. grated cheese
⅓ t. pepper

Mix celery, onion and green pepper well with steak. Add butter, salt and pepper and cook over moderate heat until meat begins to brown. Add tomato juice with noodles and simmer until noodles are tender. Cover with grated cheese.

Virginia K. Oliver

WEINER POLES

1 c. milk
¼ c. sugar
1 t. salt
¼ c. margarine
1 yeast cake
¼ c. lukewarm water
3 to 4 c. flour
2 eggs, beaten

Scald milk. Add to sugar, salt and margarine in mixing bowl. Stir well and cool. Soften yeast in the lukewarm water. Add to the rest of the ingredients. Add beaten eggs. Add flour gradually until dough is stiff enough to handle on a board. Knead until elastic and not sticky. Place dough in greased bowl, cover and leave in a warm place until double in bulk, about 1½ hours. Punch down. Shape into weiner poles. Grease a jelly roll pan or cookie sheet. Taking small to medium-sized balls, flatten and fold around each weiner. Completely seal the dough around each weiner. Line the weiner poles on the pan. Cover with wet, warm cloth. Let poles rise until double, about 45 minutes. Bake weiner poles in a 350° to 375° oven about 40 minutes or until golden brown. Remove from oven and brush with butter to keep the crust moist and soft. Serve warm or cold. Yield: 18 to 24 weiner poles.

Carol Lou Shanklin

STUFFED CABBAGE ROLLS

Mix together:

  1 lb. ground beef
  ½ lb. ground pork
  1 large onion
  2 cloves garlic, minced

Add 1 c. cooked rice

Sauce

  1 8-oz. can tomato paste
  1 12-oz. can tomato juice
  1½ t. cinnamon
    Salt and pepper
  3 T. sugar

Stir above ingredients well. Add a little sauce to meat mixture until juicy.

Put 2 medium heads of cabbage into boiling water. Remove leaves as they wilt. Put about ¼ c. meat mixture into leaves. Pour remaining sauce over rolls.

Bake in 12 x 14-inch pans at 325° for 2 hours. Do not stack the rolls. Use 2 pans. Serves 8.

Ruth Guidi

BARBECUED INDIVIDUAL MEAT LOAVES

  3 strips bacon, cut fine
  ½ c. dry bread crumbs
  ½ c. evaporated milk
  1 egg
  2 t. salt
  2 T. chopped onion
  1½ lb. ground beef chuck
  ½ lb. lean ground pork

Combine all ingredients and blend well. Shape into 7 or 8 small individual meat loaves or rolls and place on a shallow oiled baking pan.

Barbecue Sauce

  ½ c. catsup
  ½ c. vinegar
  1 T. Worcestershire sauce
  1 t. chili powder
  2 T. chopped onion

Mix all together and heat. Pour over unbaked meat loaves and bake 45 minutes in a 350° oven. Baste with sauce occasionally.

Margaret DeHass

HAM-CHEESE-OLIVE ROLL-UPS

¾ c. ripe olives
1 pkg. frozen chopped spinach
1 c. creamed cottage cheese, sieved
1 egg, slightly beaten
2 T. sliced green onion
1 t. caraway seed
½ t. Worcestershire sauce
12 thin slices smoked ham
1 10½-oz. can cheddar cheese soup
⅓ c. milk

Cut olives into wedges. Cook spinach and drain well. Combine ½ c. olives, spinach, cottage cheese, egg, onion, caraway seed and Worcestershire sauce. Spread about 2 T. of the mixture onto each ham slice, roll ham slice like jelly roll. Place ham rolls in a shallow baking dish. Cover and bake in a 350° oven for 20 minutes.

Combine soup and milk in a saucepan. Stir in remaining olives. Heat. Arrange ham rolls on serving platter, pour cheese sauce over top. Makes 6 servings.

Mrs. Melva McPhail

CHILI LIVERS

8 slices bacon
1 lb. liver, sliced
2 T. flour
1 10½-oz. can condensed onion soup
¼ c. chili sauce or catsup

Cook bacon until crisp. Remove from pan, drain and crumble. Dust liver with flour; brown in bacon drippings. Add bacon and remaining ingredients. Cover. Simmer 30 minutes or until tender. Uncover. Cook for a few minutes to thicken sauce. Makes 4 servings.

Cindy Sabby

BROILED BREADED PORK CHOPS

6 boneless pork chops (1-inch thick)
3 eggs, beaten
 Salt and pepper
2½ T. olive oil
¼ c. grated parmesan cheese
½ c. seasoned bread crumbs
3 T. butter, melted
 Juice of 1 lemon
1 garlic clove, split
 Dash of tabasco
¼ t. cayenne

Dip chops into eggs, then into bread crumbs. Do twice. Then sprinkle salt and pepper over chops. Put chops in a lightly greased broiler pan, about 8 inches from heat. Broil slowly for 10 minutes. Mix all other ingredients to make a basting sauce. When well blended discard garlic. Spoon half of the sauce over chops. Bake at 350° 25 minutes longer. Turn chops over and spoon remaining sauce over them. Bake slowly for 30 more minutes. Serves 4 to 6.

Ruth Guidi

CANTONESE SPARERIBS

4 lb. country-style spareribs
¾ c. soy sauce
¼ c. water
1 c. orange marmalade
½ t. garlic powder
¼ t. black pepper
1 T. vinegar

Cut spareribs into serving pieces. Rub with a light covering of curry powder. Place in large casserole or baking dish. Cover with 1 small chopped onion.

Combine the remaining ingredients in a saucepan. Bring to a boil, uncovered, and watch closely. Pour over ribs. Marinate overnight or a full day (24 hours).

The ribs may be baked in the pan right in the marinade. Just put the cold dish in the unheated oven and turn on the oven to 350°. Bake until tender. Or the ribs and marinade can be cooked on top of the stove over medium heat. The meat takes 1 hour or longer.

Mr. & Mrs. Richard Davis

24

PORTUGUESE BOATMAN'S STEW

2 lb. whitefish
2 onions, sliced
¼ c. vegetable oil
1 6-oz. can tomato paste
3 c. water
¼ t. red pepper
¼ t. pepper
1 c. finely chopped parsley
⅓ c. dry white wine
　Slices of Italian bread
　Salt

Cut fish in large chunks. Sprinkle with ½ t. salt. Let stand 1 hour. Lightly brown onion in oil, pour off fat. Stir in tomato paste, water, red pepper, 1½ t. salt, pepper, parsley and wine. Simmer 30 minutes. Add fish. Simmer about 10 more minutes or just until fish flakes easily with a fork. To serve, place a slice of bread in each soup bowl. Ladle stew over bread.

Edith Pikelny

CRABMEAT SOUFFLÉ

¼ c. flour
¼ t. salt
⅛ t. white pepper
3 T. margarine
1 c. milk
3 egg yolks
1 c. cooked crabmeat, flaked
1 t. lemon juice
3 egg whites, stiffly beaten

Make a white sauce of the margarine, flour, salt, pepper and milk. Set aside to cool and when cool stir in egg yolks. Mix in the crabmeat and lemon juice. Fold in egg whites. Place in ungreased baking dish (or loaf pan) and bake at 350° for 45 minutes, or until a knife comes out clean when inserted into the center.

Suzanna C. Bascochea

GULF COAST BAKED OYSTERS

1 c. diced celery
1 large onion, chopped
　Butter
1 qt. oysters, well drained
2 eggs, beaten
　Salt and pepper
　Worcestershire sauce
　Cracker crumbs (about ¼ lb.)

Sauté celery and onion slowly in butter in large skillet; add oysters. Increase heat; cook only until edges of oysters curl. Remove skillet from heat; add eggs, stirring constantly. Crumble crackers into mixture until excess moisture is absorbed. Season to taste with salt, pepper and Worcestershire sauce. Pour into greased casserole. Cover with crumbs and dot with butter. Bake, uncovered, at 350° for 30 minutes. Yield: 6 servings.

Mrs. Ralph Frazier

SEAFOOD GUMBO

3 slices bacon	1 qt. okra
1 large onion	1 qt. shrimp or
1 can tomato sauce	crayfish
1 can hot tomatoes	1 can crabmeat
1 qt. water	6 T. flour
Salt	6 T. shortening

Chop bacon and fry. Sauté onion in bacon grease. Add ingredients as listed except flour and shortening. Melt shortening in small skillet, and brown flour in this shortening. Add deeply browned flour mixture to gumbo. Stir. Let simmer until okra is tender. Serve over rice. Serves 10 to 12.

Mrs. Stan Johnson

RED FLANNEL HASH

To ½ pkg. salt cod (soaked to remove as much of the salt as possible), add 2 c. mashed potatoes, cooked beets, and onion to taste. Spread out in frying pan and brown on both sides.

Mrs. Julius Abegg

TUNA LOAF

1¼ c. milk
1 egg, beaten
1 t. instant onion
¼ c. uncooked cream of wheat

Add milk to egg. Stir in last 2 ingredients. Let stand. Meanwhile mix together:

1 6½-oz. can tuna
1 t. lemon juice
¼ t. salt
Dash of pepper
1 c. canned peas, drained

Combine with cream of wheat mixture and pour into greased loaf pan. Top with crushed cracker crumbs. Bake 1 hour at 350°. Serve plain or with a cream soup sauce. Makes 4 or 5 servings.

Mrs. David O. Sabby

SALMON PUFFS

1 tall can salmon
1 egg
½ c. flour
Small amount of minced onion
1 t. baking powder

Pour juice of salmon into cup. Mix egg with salmon. Add flour and mix well. Add onion. Add baking powder to juice; stir until foamy and then mix with salmon. Drop by teaspoon into hot grease. Fry until golden brown. (Cook within 15 minutes after adding the juice to salmon.)

Helen Foreman

RECIPES

I've gathered countless recipes
And tested many too,
But somehow I rely upon
The old ones, tried and true.

The clippings that I daily cut
Are neatly put aside
For future days...and then I find
They're still unused...untried.

Perhaps some day I'll find the time
To test each one with care,
But I've a feeling that they'll still
Be gathering dust somewhere.

Carice Williams

SWEET-SOUR FISH FILLETS

1 lb. fish fillets
1 egg, beaten
1 T. flour
2 T. salad oil
3 T. prepared yellow mustard
2 T. sugar
1 T. vinegar
¼ t. salt
½ c. chopped celery
¼ c. finely chopped onion

Cut fillets in 2-inch pieces. Mix egg and flour; dip fillets into mixture. Cook over medium heat in hot oil until browned and fish flakes easily with a fork. Combine remaining ingredients. Pour over fish and bring to a boil. Simmer, uncovered, 5 minutes. Serve on rice if desired. Serves 4.

Mrs. George W. Thompson

CREOLE SHRIMP

2 lb. fresh shrimp
  (or 3 5¾-oz. cans)
1 bay leaf
1 stalk celery with leaves, cut in pieces
1 t. pickling spice
1 T. vinegar

Cover shrimp with boiling water and add rest of ingredients. Cook 15 minutes or until tender. Drain, cover with cold water, remove shells and dark veins. Sprinkle with salt.

1 large onion, chopped
1 clove garlic, minced
2 T. salad oil
3½ c. tomatoes
1 bay leaf
2 c. cooked rice
Dash of thyme
Dash tabasco sauce
Salt and pepper

Brown onion, garlic and celery in oil. Add tomatoes and seasoning. Cook slowly for 40 minutes. Add shrimp and cook 10 minutes. Shape rice mold, hollow center, fill with shrimp mixture. Serves 6 to 8.

Doc Kingsley

TUNA-RICE DISH

  1 6-oz. can chunk-style tuna, drained
  2 c. cooked rice
  1 T. chopped onion
  1 T. lemon juice
  ½ t. salt
  2 eggs, beaten
  ¾ c. milk
  1 c. finely crushed cornflakes
  ⅓ c. grated cheese

Combine tuna, rice, onion, lemon juice, salt, eggs, milk and half of the cornflakes. Put into a 2-quart casserole which has been well buttered. Top with remaining cornflake crumbs and the cheese. Bake 30 minutes in a 350° oven.

Mabel White Epling

SHRIMP SALAD

  2 pkg. lemon or lime gelatin
  2 small cans tomato sauce (hot)
  ½ c. finely chopped onion
  1 small can shrimp
  ½ c. finely chopped celery
  2 c. boiling water

Mix gelatin in hot water, add tomato sauce. Cool, then add remaining ingredients. Chill. Serve squares of gelatin on lettuce leaf with a dash of mayonnaise on top and a small sprinkle of paprika.

Leietta M. Taylor

CHOCOLATE BANANA BREAD

2 c. sifted self-rising flour
2/3 c. sugar
1/2 c. semisweet chocolate chips
1 c. mashed bananas (about 2 medium)
1/2 c. pecans, chopped
1/3 c. melted shortening or oil
2 eggs

Sift together flour and sugar. Stir in pecans and chocolate chips. Blend bananas, eggs, and shortening or oil. Add to flour mixture and mix until flour is moistened. Turn into greased 4½ x 8½-inch loaf pan. Bake in 350° oven about 1 hour and 10 minutes, or until cake tester inserted in center comes out clean. Cool 20 minutes before removing from pan. Cool completely before slicing. Can be frozen.

Virginia Kraegenbrink

CHEESE BREAD

2 pkgs. active dry yeast
1½ c. warm water
2 T. sugar
2¼ t. salt
4¼ to 5½ c. flour
2 eggs, beaten
2 c. grated extra-sharp cheddar cheese

Sprinkle yeast on warm water. Add sugar, salt and 2 c. flour, then eggs and cheese. Beat well. Add remaining flour, using hands if necessary. Knead lightly in the bowl. Let stand 10 minutes, covered. Divide into 2 loaves and let rise until doubled in bulk. Bake at 350° about 45 minutes. Keep in pan for 10 minutes before removing.

Lynn Fleming

CARROT BREAD

¾ c. cooking oil
1 c. sugar
2 eggs
1½ c. flour
¼ t. salt
1 t. soda
1 t. cinnamon
1 c. grated carrots
1 c. chopped dates
1 c. chopped nuts

Beat oil, sugar and eggs well. Add the flour, salt, soda and cinnamon in thirds with grated carrots. Always mix well after each addition. Add the dates and the nuts. Bake in a loaf pan at 350° for 1 hour or until done.

Mrs. Earl France

APPLESAUCE NUT BREAD

2 c. all-purpose flour
¾ c. sugar
3 t. baking powder
1 t. salt
½ t. soda
½ t. cinnamon
1 c. coarsely chopped walnuts
1 egg, beaten
1 c. medium-thick smooth applesauce
2 T. melted shortening

Sift together dry ingredients. Add chopped nuts. In mixing bowl beat egg, add applesauce and melted shortening. Add dry ingredients. Stir until blended. Pour into greased loaf pan. Bake in moderate 350° oven 1 hour. Cool on rack.

Mrs. N. C. Kitchin

YEAST BISCUITS

½ cake yeast
1 c. buttermilk, warm
2½ c. flour
½ t. soda
4 T. sugar
½ t. salt
6 T. shortening

Dissolve yeast in the buttermilk. Add ingredients quickly and knead on floured board. Roll ¼-inch thick and cut. Brush with melted butter, place second half on top. Let rise 1½ to 2 hours and bake about 20 minutes at 350° or 400°.

Mrs. W. R. Brothers

EASTER BREAD

½ c. sugar
¼ lb. margarine or butter
1 whole egg
2 egg yolks
1 c. milk (scalded and cooled)
4 c. flour
1 t. lemon rind
1 t. salt
¾ c. raisins

Dissolve 1 packet dry yeast in ¼ c. luke-warm water.

Cream margarine or butter, add sugar and eggs. Mix well. Add lemon rind and salt, mix. Sift in the 4 c. flour, then add the yeast mixture and milk all at one time and mix with a wooden spoon until dough will not cling to it. Lastly, work in the raisins and let dough rise until double in bulk. Then turn out on floured board and knead. Form to make a round bread. If desired, make a twist — section it into 8 pieces, braiding 3 and 3 and 2 for the top. Grease pans. Bake in a 350° oven for about 30 minutes or until brown.

Mrs. F. K. Soucek

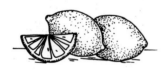

DILLY BREAD

1 pkg. yeast	1 T. instant
1 c. cottage cheese	onion
5 T. sugar	2 t. dill seed
1 T. butter	1 t. salt
1 egg	¼ t. soda
¼ c. warm water	2½ c. flour
(100°)	

Combine warm water and yeast. Heat cottage cheese to lukewarm and combine sugar, instant onion, dill seed, salt, butter, soda and egg. Add to yeast mixture. Add 2¼ to 2½ c. flour and let stand until doubled, about 1 hour. Then knead. Shape into 1 loaf and put in greased pan. Let rise again for 30 minutes and put in 350° oven for 40 to 50 minutes. Grease top of loaf after lifting from pan.

Mrs. Leo Santerre

CRUNCHY CHEESE BISCUITS

½ c. margarine
1 c. plain flour
½ t. salt
1 c. rice cereal
1 c. grated extra-sharp cheddar cheese
Tabasco or cayenne pepper to taste

Margarine and cheese should be at room temperature. Blend all ingredients together by hand until thoroughly mixed. Work in the dry cereal. Pinch off tiny balls. Place on ungreased baking sheet, press down with fork and bake at 325° about 10 minutes. Do not brown.

Mary Cunnyngham

TOMATO BUFFET BREAD

2 c. tomato juice
¼ c. tomato catsup
2 T. butter or margarine
1 t. salt
3 T. sugar
1 pkg. active dry yeast
¼ c. warm water
7 c. sifted flour

Heat tomato juice and butter together until butter is melted. Add sugar, salt and catsup. Cool to lukewarm. Sprinkle yeast on warm water, stir to dissolve. Add tomato mixture and 3 c. flour to yeast. Beat with electric mixer at medium speed 2 minutes, scraping bowl occasionally, or beat by hand until smooth.

Mix in remaining flour, a little at a time (first with a spoon and then with hands) to make a soft dough that leaves the sides of the bowl. Turn onto lightly floured board and knead until smooth and elastic, 8 to 10 minutes. Place in lightly greased bowl, turn dough over to grease top, cover and let rise in warm place until doubled, 1 to 1½ hours. Punch down and divide in half. Cover and let stand 10 minutes. Shape into loaves and place in greased 9 x 5 x 3-inch pans. Cover and let rise until almost double, about 1 hour. Bake in 425° oven about 25 minutes, or until bread tests done. Makes 2 loaves.

Johnielu Barber Bradford

TASTY BREAD OF MEXICO

1 c. yellow cornmeal
½ t. soda
1 c. milk
1 large onion, chopped
1 small can creamed corn
½ t. salt
2 eggs
⅓ c. cooking oil
3 hot peppers, finely cut
½ lb. sharp cheese, grated

Mix onion, cheese and peppers. Add remaining ingredients. Mix well. Bake in hot greased skillet for 45 minutes at 350°.

Virginia K. Oliver

HERB BREAD

½ to ⅔ c. soft butter
2 t. finely chopped onion
1 t. chopped fresh parsley
1 t. basil
1 t. lemon juice

Mix above ingredients together and spread on 1 loaf French bread, sliced ¾ through. Heat on cookie sheet at 250° for 25 minutes. Separate slices before serving.

Mrs. Loren McDonald

EVERLASTING BISCUITS

Bring to a boil and cool 1 qt. fresh milk. Add to milk:

1 c. mashed potatoes
1 c. sugar
2 t. salt
2 t. baking powder
½ t. soda
1 c. melted lard
1 cake yeast soaked in ½ c. cold water

Stir in enough flour to thicken to consistency of cake batter. Let rise until light, then work in enough flour to stiffness of biscuit dough. Roll out and cut like biscuits. Let rise and bake in a 400° oven 10 to 12 minutes.

Irene Moyle

DATE BREAD

2 c. sugar
3 c. flour
1½ c. boiling water
1 pkg. (2 cups) dates, chopped
1 c. chopped pecans
1 egg
1 t. salt
2 t. soda
1 T. butter
1 T. vanilla

Cover dates with *extra* boiling water. Let stand a few minutes. Mix other ingredients. Drain dates and add, with nuts, last. Place greased waxed paper in bottom of pan. Bake in a 400° oven for 15 minutes; then turn heat down to 300° and bake 1½ hours or longer. Place bread on rack 3 or 4 inches above the bottom of the oven, as it burns easily.

Mrs. John Bugbee

FRECKLED TEA BREAD

2 c. milk
1 c. sugar
1 t. salt
¼ t. mace
½ c. butter, melted
2 1-oz. yeast cakes
3 eggs, well beaten
9 c. flour
4 c. raisins
1 c. mixed fruit peels

Scald milk and add sugar, salt, mace and butter. Cool to lukewarm. Add crumbled yeast. Let stand 20 minutes. Gradually add beaten eggs and flour. Beat until smooth. Add raisins and peels. Turn out on floured board and knead until smooth and elastic. Place in large greased bowl and cover. Let rise until doubled in bulk. Divide into 2 parts, knead and place into greased loaf pans. Cover and let rise until doubled in bulk. Bake in hot 400° oven for 10 minutes; reduce heat to 350° and bake 35 minutes longer. Remove from pans. Brush with egg white. Sprinkle with coarse sugar. Slice thin and serve with cups of steaming tea.

Carice Williams

HOLIDAY FRUIT BREAD

1 lb. white raisins
½ lb. dried apricots, cut up
½ lb. dates, cut up
2 c. boiling water
2 t. soda
1 stick butter or margarine

Mix together in large bowl and let stand overnight.

Next morning take:

2 eggs
2 c. sugar
3 c. white flour
1 c. whole wheat flour
4 t. cinnamon
1 t. salt
1½ c. nutmeats

Beat well the eggs and sugar, add to the fruit mixture, and stir. Add the remaining ingredients and mix thoroughly. Grease well 3 small loaf pans and divide dough evenly. Bake 1 hour at 350°. May be wrapped and frozen for later use.

Eunice Oard

RAISIN BREAD

½ lb. shortening (half margarine, half butter)
4 c. sugar
5 eggs
4 c. liquid (half milk, half water)
11 c. sifted flour
12 t. baking powder
¼ t. salt
1½ t. vanilla
2 t. lemon extract
3 boxes raisins

Mix all ingredients in order listed. Grease and flour pans. Bake at 375° for 1 hour and 15 minutes. This recipe makes 4 loaves.

Henrietta B. Janssen

 ROLLS

ONION RYE ROLLS

2 c. milk, scalded
1 t. salt
½ c. maple syrup or honey
1 t. grated orange rind
1 t. caraway seeds (optional)
1 envelope onion soup mix
¼ c. melted shortening
2 eggs
3 packets yeast
3 c. rye flour
5 to 6 c. white flour

Dissolve yeast in ¾ c. warm water. To the scalded milk add the salt, maple syrup, grated orange rind, caraway seeds, onion soup mix and melted shortening. Cool. Then add eggs and beat well. Add yeast and rye flour and beat well. Cover and let stand 15 minutes. Then blend in white flour. Knead 8 to 10 minutes. Place in greased bowl and let rise until doubled in bulk. Punch down. Place on lightly floured board. Cover with bowl and let stand 30 minutes. Shape into buns. Place on greased cookie sheet. Let rise in a warm place about 1 to 1½ hours. Bake at 375° for 20 minutes. Makes about 1½ doz. buns.

Marion Hayes

ONE-HOUR ROLLS

2 pkg. dry yeast
1 c. warm water
1 T. sugar
1 t. salt
1 T. butter, melted
2½ to 2¾ c. non-sift flour

Mix well. Let rise 15 minutes. Shape and put on cookie sheet. Let rise about 30 minutes. Preheat oven to 425° and bake 15 minutes. After 10 minutes cover lightly with foil. Cool on a rack.

Mrs. A. B. Babcock

POTATO REFRIGERATOR ROLLS

¾ c. salted potato water
½ c. granulated sugar
½ c. shortening
½ c. lukewarm water
1 t. granulated sugar
1 envelope active dry yeast
2 eggs, well beaten
4½ c. presifted all-purpose flour

Heat potato water (drained from boiled potatoes) and stir in the ½ c. sugar and shortening. Cool to lukewarm. Meantime measure lukewarm water into a large bowl; stir in the 1 t. sugar. Sprinkle with yeast. Let stand 10 minutes, then stir well. Stir in lukewarm potato water mixture, eggs and 2¼ c. of the flour. Beat until smooth and elastic. Work in sufficient additional flour to make soft dough, 2¼ cups. Knead dough lightly in bowl. Cover bowl closely and refrigerate until needed. (Dough will keep 2 or 3 days.)

To bake a dozen fresh rolls: Punch dough down and cut into two equal portions. Return one portion to refrigerator. Allow other portion to come to room temperature in a warm place. Knead on floured board until smooth. Form into a 12-inch roll. Cut roll into twelve 1-inch pieces. Shape each piece into a smooth ball. Arrange, well apart, on greased cookie sheet or pan. Grease tops and cover. Let rise in a warm place, free from draft, until double in bulk — about 1 hour. Bake in a 375° oven for 12 to 15 minutes.

Lynn Snedeker

ABBREVIATIONS

t.—teaspoon
T.—tablespoon
c.—cup
pkg.—package
pt.—pint
qt.—quart
oz.—ounce
lb.—pound

OLIE BOLLEN (Oil Balls)

2 eggs, well beaten
1 qt. scalded milk (cool to medium lukewarm)
2 cakes yeast
2 c. sugar
2½ lb. flour (or enough to make a drop batter)
1 t. salt
1½ lb. raisins

Dissolve yeast in lukewarm milk, add other ingredients and beat well. Let rise until double in bulk. Drop by tablespoons in 375° deep fat. Drain on absorbent paper. Place in bag with granulated sugar and shake. Add ½ lb. fruit mix if desired.

Mrs. Kenneth E. Coon

KITCHEN PORTRAIT

The old black range gleams cheerfully
And radiates warm glow,
The kettle singing gleefully
And in a pleasant row,
The speckled blue enamel pots
Send forth a savory steam,
While from the oven odors breathe
Sweet essence of a dream.

A portrait pleasing to the eye
Is that old kitchen stove,
Where viands of a day gone by
Were like real treasure trove.
In the skillet sizzling pork,
Potatoes, vegetables galore
Knocking loudly on their lids,
And from the oven door
The fragrance of big juicy pies,
Baked Indian pudding or a dream
Of a shortcake with wild strawberries
Smothered deep in cream.

Bright patchwork holders hanging near,
Red-fringed towel. Now arrange
The iron trivets for hot pans
On the old black kitchen range.
It's dinner time — brown castleware
On red-checked cloth in place;
Ambrosial scent of country fare
And Grandpa saying grace.

Ruth B. Field

DOUGHNUTS

TINY DOUGHNUTS

1 egg, beaten   ⅓ c. buttermilk
½ c. sugar   2 c. sifted flour
½ t. salt   ¼ t. nutmeg

Mix all ingredients together, forming a soft dough. Chill at least 1 hour. Roll thin and cut with small doughnut cutter about 1½ inches across. Fry in 350° deep fat or oil until brown.

Mary Cunnyngham

To sour sweet milk, add 2 tablespoons of white vinegar to 1 cup of sweet milk and presto! sour milk or "buttermilk" for cooking!

BUTTERMILK DOUGHNUTS

2 eggs
¾ c. sugar
½ c. buttermilk
3 T. melted shortening
2 to 2¾ c. flour
1 t. baking powder
½ t. baking soda
1 t. nutmeg

Beat eggs until thick and lemon-colored. Beat in sugar, buttermilk, shortening. Mix in sifted dry ingredients. Turn dough on well-floured board. Roll ½-inch thick into 8-inch squares. Divide in half. Let stand 20 minutes; cut in ½-inch strips (dip knife in flour to prevent sticking). Press ends together to form a circle. Fry in 375° deep fat until golden brown. Turn circles as they rise to top (3 minutes). Makes about 3½ doz. doughnuts.

Eleanor Steffen

DOWN-HOME PANCAKES

  1 egg, well beaten
1¼ c. buttermilk
  ½ t. soda
1¼ c. all-purpose flour
  1 t. sugar
  1 t. baking powder
  ½ t. salt
  2 T. melted shortening

To the egg, beat in buttermilk and soda. Sift together the dry ingredients. Add the shortening. Beat until smooth.

Heat griddle until water sprinkled on top dances across the griddle. Cook on high temperature. Pour maple syrup over pancakes.

Maple Syrup

  4 c. sugar
  2 c. water
  ½ c. light syrup

Cook until syrup has a little body, then add maple flavoring to taste.

Mary A. Robinson

BUCKWHEAT CAKES

2 c. buckwheat flour
2 t. sugar
2 heaping T. cornmeal
1½ t. salt
¼ cake compressed yeast (dissolved in tepid water)
3¼ c. warm water (including above)

Mix meal, buckwheat, salt, sugar, thoroughly with water before adding dissolved yeast. Stir in gently, cover, set in warm place to lighten overnight. Next day add:

1 T. molasses
1 t. baking powder
Pinch of soda

Stir gently. Add a little warm water if too stiff. Cook on hot griddle. Serve with melted butter and syrup.

Mrs. William D. Cecil

WILD RICE PANCAKES

Wash ¼ c. wild rice several times in cold water. Cover with cold water and bring to a boil. Drain. Repeat this procedure 3 times. Add ¼ t. salt the last time and cook about 15 minutes.

1 egg, well beaten
1¼ c. buttermilk or sour milk
½ t. soda
1¼ c. flour
2 T. sugar
2 T. soft shortening
1 t. baking powder
¾ t. salt

Add buttermilk and soda to the beaten egg. Then add the remaining ingredients. Add rice to the batter. Grease griddle if necessary and spoon batter on preheated griddle. Turn when bubbles appear.

Mrs. George V. Nelson

POTATO PANCAKES

4 medium-size potatoes, grated
1 egg, well beaten
½ to ¾ c. cracker meal
Salt and pepper to taste
Dash of onion salt

Mix well and drop by spoonful into a hot, well-greased pan. Fry on both sides until golden brown. Serve with syrup.

Donna Kingsley

BUCKWHEAT CAKES

Bring them to me served with bacon,
Piled up high and steaming hot,
Bring a thrill of real enjoyment,
Just a wealth of sheer delight;
And my troubles seem forgotten
With each tantalizing bite.
You may boast of favorite dishes
That a good cook undertakes;
But I cast my vote with fervor
For a stack of buckwheat cakes.

H. Howard Biggar

PIKELETS

2 eggs
3 T. sugar
1½ c. flour
½ t. soda
¾ t. cream of tartar
Pinch of salt
¾ c. milk

Beat eggs and sugar a few minutes. Then add rest of ingredients. Heat a skillet on stove to about 300°, and turn down to 200° when cooking pikelets. Put a tablespoon of batter for each pikelet and cook until the batter bubbles a little. Turn and cook other side. Makes about 2½ doz. pikelets.

Millie Rutter

MUFFINS

BANANA MUFFINS

2 c. sifted all-purpose flour
2 t. baking powder
1 t. salt
1½ t. cinnamon
⅓ c. white sugar
1 egg, beaten
1 c. milk
¼ c. melted shortening
1 c. mashed ripe bananas

Sift flour, baking powder, cinnamon, salt and sugar into a mixing bowl. Combine beaten egg and milk, melted shortening and bananas and add all at once to flour mixture, stirring only until dry ingredients are moistened. The batter will be lumpy. Fill greased muffin tins ⅔ full. Sprinkle top of each with a mixture of 1 T. white sugar and ¼ t. cinnamon. Bake at 400° for 25 minutes.

Mrs. Hugh Morenz

OATMEAL MUFFINS

1½ c. flour   ¾ c. oatmeal
¼ c. sugar   1 egg, beaten
½ t. salt   1 c. milk
  4 t. baking powder   3 T. melted
½ c. raisins   shortening

Mix and sift flour, sugar, salt and baking powder. Add cereal, egg, milk and shortening. Beat well and pour into greased muffin tins. Bake 15 to 20 minutes in 400° oven. Makes 9 large muffins.

Margaret Goughnour

SPECIAL BLEND

Mix together ¼ c. flour and ½ c. shortening. Place in a jar and store on shelf. Use this mixture to grease and flour cake pans, muffin tins and cookie sheets.

Mrs. Sherman R. Lacy

CRANBERRY-ORANGE MUFFINS

2 c. sifted all-purpose flour
½ t. salt
1½ t. baking powder
½ t. soda
¼ c. sugar
1 c. cranberry relish
2 T. butter or margarine
⅔ c. boiling water
1 egg, beaten

Sift flour, salt, baking powder, soda and sugar together. Add butter to boiling water. Add with beaten egg to dry ingredients. Mix well together. Add the relish, mix. Spoon into well-greased muffin tins. Bake at 425° for 40 to 45 minutes. Makes 12 medium-sized muffins.

Jean Stephenson

AN OLD-FASHIONED KITCHEN

The way to face life's problems
Was learned at my mother's knee,
It was in our old-fashioned kitchen,
The center of life to me.

I learned all about truth and love,
To measure and cook with care,
To cope with the mixing of a cake,
To always be kind and share.

I learned about life and people,
To put in a pinch of herbs,
To sew a straight seam in life,
To read and all of my verbs.

This you can learn from your mother,
To face life without a doubt;
So, take pride in your kitchen,
That is what life's all about.

Polly Perkins

GERMAN CHOCOLATE CAKE

2½ c. sifted cake flour
4 eggs, separated
1 bar German chocolate
(dissolved in ½ c. hot water)
¼ t. salt
2 c. sugar
1 c. shortening
1 c. buttermilk
1 t. soda
1 t. vanilla

Beat egg whites until stiff. Set aside. Cream sugar and shortening, add 1 egg yolk at a time, beating after each addition. Add flour, alternate with ½ c. milk. Dissolve soda in remaining milk. Add to mixture. Add the dissolved chocolate, salt and vanilla. Lastly, fold in well-beaten egg whites. Bake in 3 layers at 350° for 40 minutes.

Filling

1 large can evaporated milk
1 c. sugar
1 c. chopped pecans
1 t. vanilla
3 egg yolks
1 stick margarine or butter
1 c. flaked coconut

Mix milk, egg yolks, vanilla, sugar and butter. Cook until thick, beat until partly cooled. Add coconut and pecans. Spread on cake.

Louise H. Davis

COFFEE FROSTING

3 T. melted butter
1 T. hot coffee
½ t. cinnamon
1 t. vanilla
1 c. powdered sugar

Beat well, let stand a few minutes. Good on cookies or spice cake.

Mrs. A. B. Babcock

POTATO CAKE

⅔ c. shortening
2 c. sugar
3 or 4 T. boiling water
⅔ c. ground chocolate
1 c. hot mashed potatoes
4 egg yolks, beaten
2 c. flour
1 t. each: cinnamon, cloves, nutmeg
2 t. baking soda
1 t. salt
1 c. walnuts
1 t. vanilla
4 egg whites, stiffly beaten

Cream shortening and sugar. Melt chocolate in the boiling water. Add melted chocolate, mashed potatoes and egg yolks to creamed mixture.

Sift dry ingredients. Add alternately to creamed mixture the dry ingredients and ½ c. milk. Add walnuts and vanilla and mix well. Lastly, add egg whites.

Grease a 10-inch iron frying pan and line with greased and floured waxed paper. Bake in 350° oven 1 hour or until a toothpick inserted in center comes out clean.

Note: This cake gets better if put aside for a few days before cutting.

Beatrice R. Cochrun

SPICE CAKE

2 c. raisins
2½ c. water
2 t. soda
2 c. granulated sugar
1 c. shortening
2 level t. salt
1 t. each: cinnamon, cloves, nutmeg, allspice
3½ c. sifted flour

Boil raisins in the water for about 5 minutes. Add rest of ingredients. Mix all together and bake approximately 1 hour at 350°.

Joyce A. Duquette

IRISH CHRISTMAS CAKE

½ lb. butter
1½ c. sugar
½ c. walnuts
3½ c. flour
 1 t. baking powder
½ c. orange juice
 1 lb. mixed candied cherries
   and pineapple
 1 lb. white seedless raisins
 1 lb. dark seedless raisins
 8 eggs
 1 leprechaun (optional)

Cream butter, sugar; add eggs, two at a time. Add juice and fruit. Add raisins washed in hot water. Add nuts. Fold in flour and baking powder. Put mixture in 2 loaf pans that have been greased and lined with brown paper. Bake at 275° for 2 hours, or until no cracking sound is heard when cake is held to the ear. This is to seal in the leprechaun and ensure a delightful new year.

Patricia Cater

ANGEL FOOD STRUDEL

2 c. flour
3 egg yolks,
  beaten
¼ c. water
2 T. vinegar
1 c. butter

Mix together by hand the flour and butter. Add egg yolks and water. Lastly, add vinegar. Divide dough into 7 balls. Refrigerate overnight.

Filling

½ lb. ground nuts
1½ c. granulated sugar
 1 box angel food cake mix
   Maraschino cherries

Mix together nuts and sugar. Prepare an angel food cake mix. Roll each ball of dough on a floured towel in a 10-inch circle. Sprinkle with sugar and nut mixture. Place 16 dabs of angel food cake batter on each circle. Place a piece of cherry on each dab. Roll dough with a towel. Seal edges. Bake at 350° for 30 minutes. When cool, ice if desired.

Mrs. Wilbur McIntosh

HERITAGE CAKE

"Faith and food have been linked together in our heritage since early biblical days. So how better to be aware of this link than to prepare a special treat, such as a daffodil-yellow cake, from biblical listings, knowing that it will not only nourish the body but also the soul."

½ c. Judges 5:25
> "...and she brought forth *butter* in a lordly dish."

1 c. Jeremiah 6:20
> "To what purpose cometh there to me incense from Sheba, and the sweet *cane* from a far country?"

3 Jeremiah 17:11
> "As the partridge sitteth on *eggs*, and hatcheth them not; so he that getteth riches, and not by right, shall leave them in the midst of his days, and at his end shall be a fool."

1 t. II Chronicles 9:9
> "And she gave the king an hundred and twenty talents of gold, and of *spices* great abundance..."

2 c. I Kings 4:22
> "And Solomon's provision for one day was thirty measures of *fine flour*."

2 t. Amos 4:5
> "And offer a sacrifice of thanksgiving with *leaven*, and proclaim and publish the free offerings..."

¼ t. Leviticus 2:13
> "...With all thine offerings thou shalt offer *salt*."

¾ c. Judges 4:19
> "And she opened a bottle of *milk*, and gave him drink, and covered him."

HERITAGE CAKE

    1 c. sugar
    ½ c. butter or margarine
    3 eggs, separated
    2 c. sifted cake flour
    2 t. double-acting baking powder
    ¼ t. salt
    1 t. grated lemon rind
    ⅛ t. nutmeg
    ¾ c. milk

All ingredients should be at room temperature before mixing cake. Preheat oven to 375°. Prepare two 8-inch layer pans by greasing lightly and dusting with flour.

Soften butter in a large mixing bowl. Add sugar gradually, creaming until daffodil yellow. Add 3 egg yolks, beating until mixture is light. Resift flour with baking powder, salt and nutmeg. Add lemon rind. Stir to blend. Add flour mixture to butter mixture in three parts, with thirds of milk at each addition. Stir batter until smooth after each addition. Pour into prepared layer pans. Bake in preheated oven 25 minutes or until cake springs back to touch. Remove from oven and cool 10 minutes. Then turn onto rack to complete cooling. Use favorite filling and icing. Or remove one layer to cake plate and spread with ¾ c. (or more) pure raspberry jam. Cover with remaining layer. Dust this with ¼ c. sifted confectioners' sugar. Makes two 8-inch layers.

Alma Ralston

MARRIED WOMAN'S CAKE

    1 lb. true love
    1 lb. perfect trust and confidence
    Pinch of unselfishness
    Sprinkle of interest in all he does

Mix all with a gill of oil of sympathy. Flavor with a bright fireside and a loving kiss. Bake well all your life.

Irene Moyle

JAM CAKE

5 eggs	2 t. soda
1½ c. butter	1 t. allspice
2½ c. sugar	½ t. cloves
2 c. jam	½ t. pepper
1 c. buttermilk	1 T. cinnamon
4 c. flour	

Cream butter and sugar until light and fluffy. Add eggs one at a time and beat until creamy. Sift flour, soda and spices together. Add to creamed mixture alternately with milk, beating after each addition. Fold in jam. Bake in 3 greased and floured layer cake pans in a 300° oven until cake tests done. Cool. Spread Caramel Icing between layers and on sides of cake.

Caramel Icing

3 c. sugar	1 c. milk
1 c. butter	1 c. sugar

Mix sugar, milk and butter in a heavy saucepan. Bring to a quick boil. Place 1 c. sugar in an iron skillet and cook to a light-brown syrup, stirring constantly. After the sugar has browned, pour into boiling mixture, stirring constantly. Cook until icing reaches the soft-ball stage. Remove from heat and beat until icing is lukewarm. Spread on cake.

Elizabeth Wilson

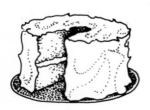

OVEN FROSTING

1 c. cream
2 c. coconut
2 c. white sugar or brown sugar
1 c. nuts

Mix together and cook in oven. Frosting is enough for a 9 x 13-inch cake.

E. Johnson

CHIFFON CAKE

2 c. flour	1 c. buttermilk
2 c. sugar	2 eggs
2 t. soda	2 t. vanilla
1 t. salt	1 c. vegetable oil
½ c. cocoa	1 c. hot water

Mix ingredients in order listed, except hot water. When well mixed add hot water. Mix well.

Bake in angel food cake pan in 350° oven. Cake is done when it pulls from sides of pan.

Mrs. C. E. Mathews

LEMON RHUBARB CAKE

Prepare 1 box lemon cake mix. Put into 9 x 13-inch pan. Sprinkle 2 c. finely cut rhubarb over cake. Sprinkle 1½ c. sugar over rhubarb. Sprinkle one 3-oz. box strawberry gelatin over all. Bake 50 to 60 minutes at 350°.

Gertrude Hogate

SOUR CREAM POUND CAKE

2 c. sugar	¼ t. soda
½ lb. butter	2 c. plain flour
4 eggs	1 t. vanilla
1 c. grated coconut	1 c. sour cream

Cream butter and 1½ c. sugar. Add two egg yolks at a time until well mixed. Mix in coconut and vanilla. Sift soda and flour and add alternately with sour cream. Beat egg whites until stiff, adding the remaining ½ c. sugar. Fold egg whites into batter and mix well. Bake in tube pan at 200° until well browned.

Mrs. A. W. Lockwood

WORLD WAR I CAKE

2 T. lard	¼ t. cloves, ground
1 c. sugar	
1 c. water	¼ t. nutmeg
½ c. raisins	½ t. salt
1 t. cinnamon	

Combine above ingredients. Boil together 10 minutes. Cool. Then add 2 c. flour and ¾ t. baking soda. Bake at 350° until done.

Patricia Mongeau

APPLE OR PEACH KUCHEN

Sliced apples or peaches
1¼ c. sifted all-purpose flour
1 t. baking powder
1 T. sugar
¼ t. salt
½ c. butter or margarine
1 small egg, slightly beaten
2 T. milk

In a large bowl sift together flour, baking powder, sugar and salt. Add butter, egg and milk. Cut in as in making piecrust. Spread batter into a 9-inch-square greased baking pan (batter is stiff and spreads best by using the fingertips). Place fruit slices in lines overlapping each other, completely covering batter. Sprinkle topping over peaches or apples. Bake in a 350° oven for 35 to 45 minutes or until sugar melts and becomes syrupy. Eat warm or cold.

Topping

¾ c. sugar
1½ T. flour
½ t. cinnamon
2 T. butter

Mix topping until blended.

Mrs. P. Jezick

WALNUT HONEY LOAF

1 c. honey
1 c. milk
½ c. sugar
2½ c. sifted flour
1 t. soda
1 t. salt
½ c. chopped walnuts
¼ c. shortening
1 egg

Combine honey, milk and sugar in 3-quart saucepan. Stir over medium heat until sugar is dissolved. Cool. Sift together flour, soda and salt. Add dry ingredients, nuts, shortening and egg to cooled mixture and beat 2 minutes or 300 strokes by hand. Turn into greased and floured 9 x 5-inch loaf pan. Bake at 325° for 1¼ hours to 1½ hours or until cake tester comes out clean. Cool 15 minutes. Remove from pan and cool on rack. Makes 1 loaf.

Emma Dredla

SAUSAGE CAKE

1 lb. pork sausage
1½ c. firmly packed brown sugar
1½ c. sugar
2 eggs, slightly beaten
3 c. sifted flour
1 t. ginger
1 t. baking powder
1 t. pumpkin pie spice
1 t. baking soda
1 c. cold strong coffee
1 c. chopped walnuts
1 c. raisins

Combine meat and sugars, stir until well blended. Add eggs and beat well. Sift flour, ginger, baking powder and pumpkin pie spice onto waxed paper. Stir baking soda into coffee. Add flour mixture and coffee alternately to meat mixture, beating well after each addition. Pour boiling water over raisins, let stand 5 minutes. Drain. Fold raisins and walnuts into cake batter. Pour into greased and floured tube cake pan. Bake 1½ hours at 350°.

Edna Wagner

QUEEN ELIZABETH CAKE

¼ c. butter
1 egg, beaten
1½ c. all-purpose flour
1 c. dates
1 c. boiling water
1 t. baking powder
1 t. soda
¼ t. salt
1 c. white sugar
1 t. vanilla

Pour boiling water over chopped dates and let stand until cool. Mix all together and bake about 35 minutes at 350° in 8-inch square pan.

Praline Icing

10 T. brown sugar
3 T. butter
3 T. cream

Boil about 3 minutes and add about ½ c. coconut and ½ c. chopped nuts. Spread on baked warm cake and put under broiler for a few minutes until bubbly.

Mrs. Hugh Morenz

MARSHMALLOW FUDGE CAKE

1 c. margarine
2½ c. sugar
4 sq. semisweet chocolate, melted
4 eggs, beaten
1 c. flour
¼ t. salt
1 t. vanilla
1 bag miniature marshmallows
1 c. nuts

Cream butter and sugar. Add beaten eggs, chocolate, vanilla, flour, salt and nuts. Pour into a greased loaf pan. Bake about 45 minutes in a 350° oven. (Cake will sink somewhat in the middle). Remove from oven and sprinkle marshmallows over cake. Return to oven for 1 minute. Remove and pat lightly with hand to smooth marshmallows over cake.

Fudge Icing

2 c. sugar
½ c. milk
¼ c. corn syrup
½ c. cocoa
1 stick margarine
1 t. vanilla
Pinch of salt
½ c. nuts

Mix cocoa and sugar. Gradually add milk, syrup and butter. Cook over medium heat until soft ball forms (approximately 12 to 15 minutes). Remove and cool 20 minutes. Add salt and vanilla and nuts. Beat and spread over cake.

Mrs. Jimmy Cunningham

RED BUTTERMILK CAKE

1½ c. sugar	2 t. cocoa
½ c. butter	1 t. salt
2 eggs	1 c. buttermilk
2 oz. red food	2½ c. cake flour
coloring	1 t. vinegar
1 t. vanilla	1 t. soda

Cream shortening; add eggs and sugar and beat with electric mixer until light and fluffy (so none of the sugar grains can be felt with fingers).

Make a paste of cocoa and food coloring and add to above. Add salt to flour and add with buttermilk. Then add vanilla. Beat 8 to 10 minutes. Mix soda and vinegar and blend in at low speed (do not beat hard after vinegar has been added). Pour into three 9-inch pans. Bake 30 minutes at 350°.

Icing

5 T. flour	1 c. sugar
2 t. sugar	1 c. butter
1 c. milk	1 t. vanilla

Mix flour with 2 t. sugar. Add milk. Cook until thick. Cream the next 3 ingredients until light (15 minutes). When it takes on the appearance of whipped cream, add flour mixture by small teaspoonsful. Whip until like whipped cream.

Mildred Ashley

RUM CAKE

1⅓ c. sugar	1 t. vanilla
½ lb. butter	2 t. rum extract
2 c. sifted flour	4 eggs

Cream sugar and butter. Add eggs and beat. Add sifted flour and extracts and beat well. Bake in greased and floured angel food cake pan 1 hour at 325°.

Glaze

Cook 1 c. sugar, ½ c. water, ½ t. each rum and butter flavorings for 5 minutes. Allow to cool. Pour over warm cake.

Helen Washburn

SLAVE CAKE

"This cake recipe was handed down from slave days in the South."

- 5 egg whites
- 2 c. sugar
- 1 c. sour milk
- 3 c. flour
- 3 level t. baking powder
- 1 c. butter
- 1 t. vanilla
- 1 t. lemon extract

Beat sugar and butter together until creamy. Sift flour and baking powder together 4 times. Gradually add sour milk and beat until smooth. Flavor with vanilla and lemon extracts. Bake in square, round or rectangular pan in 350° oven 45 minutes. Cool, then ice.

Stella Craft Tremble

For a quick'n easy frosting, beat 1 egg white until foamy; add 1 cup sugar and ½ cup pineapple juice. Whip in electric beater at high speed 7 to 10 minutes or until it stands in peaks.

SALTED PEANUT CAKE

- 1 c. white sugar
- ½ c. shortening
- 2 egg yolks
- 1 c. ground salted peanuts
- 1 c. sour milk
- 1 t. soda
- 1½ c. flour
- 1 t. vanilla

Mix above ingredients in order listed. Pour in prepared 9 x 13-inch cake pan. Bake at 350° until done. Frost as desired or use the following frosting.

Frosting

- 2 egg whites
- 4 T. cold water
- ¼ t. cream of tartar
- ¾ c. white sugar
- ¾ c. brown sugar

Boil in double boiler 7 minutes.

Nancy Sandretto

VALENCIA ORANGE VELVET PIE

1 chocolate cookie pie shell
1 c. hot water
1 pkg. orange gelatin
¼ c. fresh Valencia orange juice
¼ c. crushed pineapple
⅛ t. salt
2 T. lemon juice
1 T. grated orange peel
1 c. heavy cream (or 6 oz. cream cheese)

Prepare chocolate cookie pie shell with a small amount of butter or cooking oil, but add no sugar to the cookie crumbs. Bake at 375° 8 to 10 minutes.

Dissolve gelatin in hot water. Add salt, lemon juice and crushed pineapple. Chill until mixture partially thickens.

In a blender whip gelatin mixture, adding the orange and cubed cream cheese or heavy cream. Pour into pie shell and chill. This sets very quickly.

Before serving, top each portion with a thin layer of sour cream and chocolate shavings or decorations.

Mr. & Mrs. Richard Davis

PEANUT BUTTER PIE

1 baked pie shell
1 c. powdered sugar
½ c. peanut butter
¼ c. cornstarch
⅔ c. sugar
¼ t. salt
3 T. butter
2 c. scalded milk
3 egg yolks, beaten
¼ t. vanilla
3 egg whites

Combine powdered sugar and peanut butter. Blend until appearance of biscuit mixture. Spread half of the mixture on baked pie shell. Combine cornstarch, sugar and salt; add scalded milk and mix well. Pour this mixture over beaten egg yolks and cook in top of double boiler until mixture thickens. Add butter and vanilla. Pour into prepared pie shell.

Beat egg whites until stiff. Spread evenly over pie filling. Sprinkle peanut butter mixture over top. Bake at 325° until brown.

Helen Foreman

ORIGINAL KEY LIME PIE

6 egg yolks, slightly beaten
1 can sweetened condensed milk
½ c. key lime juice
6 egg whites
4 T. sugar

Mix egg yolks and milk well. Add lime juice slowly to above mixture. Pour into a prebaked pie shell. Beat egg whites stiff, gradually adding sugar. Swirl meringue on pie. Bake in 300° oven about 30 minutes until meringue is light honey-colored.

Dan A. Hoover

KEY LIME PIE

On this sunny little island,
Where the warm gulf waters flow,
Grows a lime of subtle flavor
That the foremost gourmets know.
Nothing else can match its flavor,
Though the world still vainly tries
To create the taste sensation
Found only in key lime pies.

Dan A. Hoover

PIECRUST WITH EGG

4 c. flour
1¾ c. shortening
2 t. salt
1 T. sugar
1 egg, beaten with ½ c. water
1 T. vinegar

Cut together first 4 ingredients. Add egg and vinegar. Mix well, then mold. Chill at least 15 minutes before using.

This recipe can also be frozen. Separate in ¾ lb. balls and cover each with aluminum foil. Then freeze. Makes 4 good-sized pies.

Mrs. Stanley J. Wood

CRANBERRY CHIFFON PIE

1 9-inch baked piecrust
1 T. unflavored gelatin
½ c. water
⅛ t. salt
¼ c. cold water
2½ c. fresh cranberries
¾ c. sugar
2 t. grated orange rind
¼ c. orange juice
3 egg whites
6 T. sugar
½ c. whipping cream, whipped
1 t. vanilla

Soften gelatin in ¼ c. water. In a saucepan cook cranberries in ½ c. water or less, add ¾ c. sugar and salt. Cook until berries pop open. Stir occasionally. Blend in orange rind, orange juice and gelatin. Chill to thicken. (This mixture may be made the night before.) Next day whip egg whites until stiff peaks form, then gradually add sugar. Fold the whipped cream and then fold the egg whites into cranberry mixture. Pour entire mixture into baked pie shell. Chill until ready to serve.

Aurora Santerre

CHOCOLATE CHIP PIE

1¼ c. crushed graham crackers
2 T. sugar
¼ c. melted butter

To make a 9-inch graham cracker crust, blend above ingredients thoroughly in pie pan. Press mixture firmly and evenly against the bottom and sides of pan. Bake at 350° for 10 minutes. Cool.

Filling

¾ c. milk
3 T. butter
45 marshmallows
1½ sq. bitter chocolate, grated
½ c. whipping cream, whipped

Melt first 3 ingredients in a double boiler. Cool. Add chocolate and whipped cream. Put in graham cracker crust and refrigerate. Top with whipped cream and serve.

Lu Roepke

COTTAGE CHEESE PIE

1 unbaked piecrust
1 c. cottage cheese
½ c. cream
2 eggs, beaten
½ c. sugar
1 t. cornstarch

Beat eggs, add rest of ingredients. Pour in unbaked piecrust. Sprinkle with cinnamon. Bake at 350° for 35 to 40 minutes.

Mrs. Robert Petry

GLAZED CHEESE PIE

1 9-inch unbaked pie shell
1 8-oz. pkg. cream cheese
½ c. sugar
2 T. flour
2 eggs
⅓ c. milk
1 t. vanilla

Cream the cheese until soft; add sugar gradually. Stir in the flour and whole eggs and mix thoroughly. Add milk and vanilla and mix again. Pour into unbaked pie shell. Bake in a 350° oven about 40 minutes or until the mixture is set. Cool and glaze with one of the following glazes.

Pineapple Glaze

Cook together until bubbly 1 c. pineapple juice and 1 T. cornstarch mixed with 1 T. sugar. Add ½ c. drained, crushed pineapple and 1 t. vanilla. Pour over cooled pie.

Blueberry Glaze

Thaw 1 pkg. frozen blueberries. Drain juice and add mixture of 1 T. cornstarch and 1 T. sugar. Cook until thick and clear. Add 1 t. grated lemon rind and the blueberries. Pour over cooled pie.

Cherry Glaze

Use sour cherries. Cook together 1 c. cherry juice and 1 T. cornstarch mixed with 4 T. sugar. Stir in 1 t. almond extract and ½ c. cherries. Use a few drops red food coloring to keep the cherries a bright red. Pour over cooled pie.

This recipe may be doubled. Use a deep-dish 10-inch pie plate. Bake 1 hour or until the pie is set.

Catherine L. Dilks

MENNONITE DUTCH
APPLE PIE

7 apples, quartered
½ c. white sugar
½ c. brown sugar
3 T. flour
¼ pt. table cream
Butter
Cinnamon
Pastry for a 1-crust pie

Arrange apple segments around the outer edge, rounded sides up. Continue arranging in circles until pastry shell is covered. Apples may tightly touch, but not overlap. Sprinkle white sugar over apples. Mix brown sugar and flour together and sprinkle over apples. Add the cream. Dot with butter and sprinkle with cinnamon. Bake 15 minutes at 400°, then bake 20 to 25 minutes at 350° (until apples are tender).

Mrs. W. G. Pearce

MAPLE SYRUP PIE

1 c. maple syrup
1 c. hot water
2 egg yolks
1 t. butter
2 egg whites
⅛ t. salt
1 T. maple syrup

Combine 1 c. syrup, hot water and butter. Bring to a full boil. Mix cornstarch, salt and enough cold water to make a thin paste. Add egg yolks to paste and beat well. Add hot syrup mixture gradually and return to heat. Cook until thickened, stirring constantly. Cool slightly. Pour into previously baked pie shell. Beat egg whites until stiff, slowly adding the tablespoon of syrup. Pile on pie and brown golden in hot oven. Add chopped nuts if desired.

Ruth B. Field

SODA CRACKER PIE

3 egg whites, beaten stiff
1 t. baking powder
1 c. sugar
10 small soda crackers, crushed
½ c. walnuts
  Vanilla

Fold all ingredients into egg whites. Pour in greased pie tin. Bake 20 minutes at 350°. Top with ice cream and strawberries.

Esther Gjesvold

OLD-FASHIONED PIECRUST

3 c. flour   3 T. water
1 c. lard   1 T. vinegar
½ t. salt   1 whole egg

Mix the egg with water and vinegar and add to the flour which has been mixed with the lard.

Vi Spiel

PIE TIMBER

When the apple bin was getting low,
Dried fruits and preserves began to go
Like hot cakes —then Gram would say —
"Guess we won't have pie today."
But the family put up a hullabaloo,
Liked pie for dinner and supper too,
And often for breakfast in days gone by
We'd all "top off" with a wedge of pie.

My gram made many pies in her day —
They'd circle the earth —I dare not say
How many times! but in spring she'd sigh,
"Pie timber's low —well, bye and bye
The maple sap will start to run."
Then we knew a luscious pie would come
To grace Gram's table; she'd fetch the jug
Of syrup —too heavy for me to lug.

And of all the pies my grandma made,
This put the others in the shade,
For it was made of "maple honey,"
Cooked with butter and eggs till sunny,
And I'll always remember until I die
The ambrosia of Gram's maple syrup pie,
When the usual pie timber got low
And spring brought sap with the "sugar snow."

Ruth B. Field

ORANGE PECAN PIE

3 egg yolks
  Grated orange rind
½ c. sugar
1⅔ c. evaporated milk (plus orange juice to make 2¼ cups)
3 egg whites
  Pinch of salt
¼ c. pecans or walnuts

Beat egg yolks. Add orange rind, sugar, milk and orange juice. Mix well. Add salt to egg whites and beat until stiff, adding ¼ c. sugar gradually. Fold in first mixture. Pour into an unbaked pie shell and sprinkle with chopped nuts. Bake in 425° oven 10 minutes, then in a 300° oven ½ hour longer.

Wilma Johnson

EGG CUSTARD PIE

1 c. sugar
2½ T. flour
⅛ t. salt
Dash of nutmeg
4 egg yolks
1 9-inch unbaked piecrust
2 egg whites
1 c. milk
2 T. butter, melted
2 T. sugar
2 egg whites

Combine sugar, flour, salt and nutmeg. Beat the 4 egg yolks and 2 egg whites, and add to the dry ingredients. Beat well. Add milk gradually, then stir in melted butter.

Pour in crust and bake at 400° for 10 minutes. Reduce heat to 325° and bake 25 to 30 minutes longer. Beat 2 egg whites and add the 2 T. sugar. Bake meringue at 325° for 10 minutes.

Carole A. Davis

YELLOW

is buttercups and cowslips,
butterflies and honey,
forsythia and saffron
and air that's bright and sunny,
crocus and daisy eyes,
ripened wheat and mustard,
but sweetest are the egg yolks
made into sweet custard.

Roy Z. Kemp

EASY COCONUT PIE

3 eggs
1¼ c. sugar
6 T. buttermilk
6 T. melted butter
1 c. coconut
1 t. vanilla
¼ t. salt
1 9-inch unbaked pie shell

Mix all ingredients together. Pour into pie shell. Bake at 350° for 30 or 40 minutes.

Mrs. Charles Patterson

APPLE-PINEAPPLE PIE

6 medium, tart apples
½ c. crushed pineapple
¾ c. sugar
½ t. salt
1 t. lemon juice
1 t. cinnamon
¼ t. mace
2 T. butter
2 T. quick tapioca
2 T. water

Pare, core and slice apples. Mix all ingredients except butter and pour into a piecrust in large pie pan. Dot with the butter. Cover with top crust that has been pierced with a fork so steam can escape. Bake in 425° oven 15 minutes, then turn oven down to 400° and bake 25 minutes.

Sugar and a sprinkle of water may be put on top crust before baking. Browns nicely.

Piecrust

2 c. sifted flour
2 sticks margarine
Dash of salt
½ t. baking powder

Mix all together.

Louise Jackson

LEMON PIE

2 c. water
7 T. cornstarch
1¼ c. white sugar
3 egg yolks
1 T. butter
Grated rind and juice of 1 lemon
1 baked pie shell

Mix ½ c. of the water and the cornstarch to a thin paste. Combine the rest of the water and the 1¼ c. sugar and bring to a boil. Add cornstarch paste and cook until thick.

In a separate bowl mix the egg yolks and butter. Add to above mixture and cook. Add lemon and pour into pie shell. Cover with a meringue made of 3 egg whites, 1 t. lemon juice and 3 t. sugar. Bake in 375° oven for 15 minutes.

Mrs. H. Morran

GELATIN PLUM PUDDING

1 pkg. cherry gelatin
1 pt. hot water
Dash of salt
½ t. cinnamon
¼ t. cloves
¾ c. finely cut raisins
¾ c. finely cut cooked prunes
¼ c. finely cut citron
¾ c. finely cut nutmeats
¾ c. Grape Nuts

Dissolve gelatin in hot water. Add salt and spices. Chill. When slightly thickened, fold in combined fruits, nuts and Grape Nuts. Turn into large mold. Chill until firm. Unmold. Garnish with whipped cream. Makes 10 servings.

Mrs. Donald Harwood

KING ALPHONSE PUDDING

1 c. milk
¾ c. dark crème de cacao
1 4½-oz. pkg. instant chocolate pudding
    mix

Combine milk and crème de cacao in mixing bowl, then add instant pudding mix and beat at lowest speed of electric mixer until thoroughly blended. Pour into dessert glasses and chill in refrigerator for at least 3 hours. Garnish with sweetened whipped cream and freshly grated chocolate slivers. Serves 4.

Jacqueline Shafer

SWEET POTATO PUDDING

3 eggs
1½ c. sugar
1½ c. milk
½ c. butter
2 t. vanilla
⅛ t. salt
4 c. grated raw sweet potatoes
1 orange, grated

Preheat oven to 350°. Beat eggs, add milk and sugar. Melt butter and add to potatoes. Add grated orange peel. Place all ingredients in a 2-quart baking dish, stir. Bake 45 minutes.

Mildred King

MOTHER'S BEST-EVER PUDDING

½ c. brown sugar
1 egg
1 T. shortening
½ t. salt
½ c. milk
1 c. chopped dates
½ c. chopped walnuts
1½ c. flour
1½ t. baking powder

Mix in order listed. In a 9 x 13-inch cake pan, put 1 c. brown sugar and pour 1 c. boiling water over it. Stir until all sugar is dissolved. Drop batter into liquid by spoonsful. Bake 30 to 35 minutes in a 350° oven. Serve with whipped cream or any whipped topping. Serves 12 to 15.

Florence Kohle and Margaret Carnes

DATE-NUT PUDDING

1½ c. brown sugar
2 c. boiling water
1 c. chopped dates
1 c. chopped pecans
1 c. white sugar
1 c. sifted flour
1 t. baking powder
2 t. cinnamon
Dash of salt
½ c. milk
1 t. vanilla

Combine brown sugar and boiling water in 8 x 10 x 2-inch baking pan and place over low heat. Stir until sugar is dissolved. Leave mixture on burner to stay hot. Sift flour with baking powder, cinnamon and salt. Add sugar, chopped dates and nuts. Combine milk and vanilla and add to dry mixture, stirring until well mixed. Drop by spoonsful into hot mixture on burner, bake in a preheated oven at 350° for 30 minutes. Serve with whipped cream.

Mrs. John Waite

CHERRY PUDDING

1 T. butter
1 c. sugar
1 egg
1 c. sour pie cherries,
   drained (save juice)
1 c. flour
1 t. soda
⅛ t. salt
1 t. vanilla
½ c. chopped nuts

Bake at 350° for 40 minutes. Remove from oven. When cool top with the following:

¼ c. brown sugar
2 T. cherry juice
2 T. butter

Bring to boil. Let cool and then spread over top of pudding. For best flavor let stand 24 hours before serving. Add a dollop of ice cream or whipped cream.

Mary Beth Johnson

CHERRY PIE DELIGHT

1 c. pie cherries, drained
1 c. pecans, chopped
1 c. whipping cream, whipped
1 can condensed milk
   Juice of 2 lemons
1 9-inch graham cracker crust
2 T. graham cracker crumbs

Mix the lemon juice and milk. Then add pecans and cherries and fold in the whipped cream. Pour mixture into graham cracker crust, and sprinkle cracker crumbs on top. Chill before serving.

Mrs. Edward J. Herron

CHERRY DUMPLINGS

1 #2 can sour pitted cherries
1 can water
1 c. sugar

Bring to a boil and let simmer. Make a short pie dough. Roll thin. Cut into thin strips and drop into cherry mixture. Cook slowly, but do not stir. Use fork to press strips of dough into the juice. Cook until done. Serve with whipped cream or topping.

Gladys M. Chapman

FUDGE MELTAWAY BARS

½ c. butter
1 sq. chocolate
½ c. sugar
2 c. graham cracker crumbs
1 egg, beaten
1 t. vanilla
1 c. coconut
½ c. chopped nuts

Melt butter, chocolate and sugar. Add rest of ingredients. Press in 9 x 9-inch pan. Frost with ¼ c. softened butter, 2 c. confectioners' sugar, 1 t. vanilla and 1 T. milk. Top with 1½ sq. melted unsweetened chocolate.

Jean Wentz

RHUBARB DELIGHT

½ c. brown sugar
½ c. butter
2 c. flour
2 eggs
1½ t. baking powder
2 3-oz. pkg. strawberry gelatin

Mix first 5 ingredients together and pat into the bottom of a greased 13 x 9 x 2-inch pan. Wash and cut into ½-inch pieces enough rhubarb to cover crust completely. Then sprinkle gelatin powder over the rhubarb. Top with a streusel topping of ½ c. butter, 1 c. flour, 1½ c. sugar. Bake 40 minutes at 350°. Serve with ice cream or whipped cream.

Jean Maurity

Stir freshly grated orange rind into sweetened applesauce. This is a delightfully refreshing combination.

Virginia D. Young

MINTED GRAPEFRUIT

To one 16-oz. can grapefruit sections, add about 10 after-dinner mints. Chill thoroughly to blend the flavors. Serve when mints are dissolved.

June Kissinger

APPLESAUCE MOLD

2 pkg. fruit-flavored gelatin
2 c. hot water
1 c. cold water
1 c. milk
¾ c. applesauce
¼ c. chopped pecan meats
1 c. whipped cream
12 cherries

Dissolve gelatin in hot water. Add cold water, stir in applesauce and nuts. Add milk, blend well, and pour into mold. After placing in refrigerator, stir slowly every 3 or 4 minutes until mixture begins to thicken. When congealed, top with whipped cream and cherries. Serves 6.

Virginia K. Oliver

CHOCOLATE LADYFINGER ICEBOX TORTE

½ lb. butter
4 sq. German sweet chocolate
4 eggs
1 c. sugar
4 doz. ladyfingers (split in half)

Melt the chocolate over hot water. Cream butter and sugar. Add melted chocolate. Beat 20 minutes. Add 1 egg at a time and beat 5 minutes after each addition. Put ladyfingers on bottom and sides of springform pan. Alternate layers of chocolate mixture and ladyfingers to top of pan. Set aside in refrigerator. Serve with whipped cream.

Helen Punke

BUTTER TART FILLING

½ c. butter
2 c. brown sugar
1 T. vinegar
2 eggs

Melt butter and beat in brown sugar, vinegar and eggs. Use to fill unbaked tart shells. Bake 12 to 15 minutes or until golden brown.

Mrs. G. Artist

MAMA'S APPLE STRUDEL

The dough consisted of about 2 c. flour and a pinch of salt. Mama shaped this into a small hill on a floured board. In the center of the hill she poured about 3 T. melted butter, ¼ c. lukewarm water and 1 unbeaten egg white. Mixing it all with her fingers, she kneaded it into a ball and then put it in a greased mixing bowl in a warm place to set for ½ hour while she made the filling.

The filling was usually about 3 or 3½ lbs. of tart apples from our own orchard which she peeled and sliced. Then she took 1 c. sugar and added 1 t. cinnamon. Also standing by was ½ c. melted butter and 1 c. very fine bread crumbs which had been slightly browned in butter, ½ c. peeled slivered almonds, 1 c. seedless raisins, and ⅓ c. cut-up powdered-sugared dates.

She went back to the dough which she now placed on a floured board and rolled out and folded over and rolled out and stretched until it became almost paper-thin. When Mama had it the desired size, she took the melted butter, sprinkled it over the dough, followed by the buttered bread crumbs. She carefully placed the slices of apples on the dough and added the raisins, almonds, and dates and finally poured over it all the rest of the sugar-cinnamon. Dabs of butter were often put here and there. If she thought the apples were not tart enough she would squirt a few drops of lemon juice over the entire mixture.

Next to getting the dough paper-thin came the rolling up of the dough, usually in the shape of a horseshoe and gingerly placed on the greased pan. She gave it a finishing touch with a greased feather brush that had been dipped into melted butter. All of this was baked in a 350° oven for 45 to 50 minutes.

Bryne K. Brooke

ANGEL FLUFF

2 eggs
1 c. sugar
2 c. pineapple juice
1 pkg. lemon or cherry gelatin
1 large can evaporated milk
1 angel food cake

Chill evaporated milk for whipping, set aside. Beat the eggs, whip in sugar. Add pineapple juice and cook 2 to 3 minutes. Remove from heat, add gelatin. Cool. Whip the can of chilled milk, stir in custard slowly. Pour over a layer of sliced angel food cake in 13 x 9 x 2-inch dish. Place in refrigerator. Serves 18.

Mrs. Jessie Felder

CARMELITES

1⅓ c. flour
1⅓ c. oatmeal
¾ t. soda
¾ c. melted butter
1 c. brown sugar
¼ t. salt
1 egg

Press half of crust mixture into a 9 x 13-inch pan. Bake 10 minutes at 350°. Melt together 40 light caramels and 8 T. light cream. Spread over crust. Over this sprinkle 1 c. chocolate chips and ½ c. pecans or walnuts. Crumble rest of crust over this and bake 15 to 20 minutes longer. Cut into bars.

Mrs. Manford Dale

CRUMBLE CAKE

2½ c. pastry flour
1 c. brown sugar
1 c. butter

Place above ingredients in a bowl and mix until crumbly. Spread ⅓-inch thick evenly in a shallow pan. Bake in a 350° oven until a golden brown. Cut into squares while hot and remove from pan.

Ira Nethaway

CHEESE COOKIES

¼ lb. butter
1 lb. strong grated cheese
2 c. sifted flour
½ t. salt
½ t. paprika
1½ c. chopped nuts

Cream butter and cheese. Add paprika, salt and flour. Mix well. Add nuts. Shape into sausage rolls. Wrap in waxed paper. Chill several hours. Slice very thin. Bake in moderate oven about 10 minutes.

Martha Lindsey

RAISIN-PUMPKIN CRISPS

1 c. raisins
½ c. butter or margarine
1 c. sugar
1 egg
½ c. canned pumpkin
1¾ c. sifted all-purpose flour
¼ t. salt
1 t. soda
1 t. cinnamon
½ t. ginger
¾ t. nutmeg
¼ t. cloves
1 t. vanilla
½ c. coarsely chopped nuts

Rinse and drain raisins. Cream butter and sugar thoroughly. Add unbeaten egg and beat until well blended. Stir in pumpkin. Sift together flour, salt, soda and spices and add to creamed mixture. Stir in vanilla, raisins and nuts. Drop by small spoonsful onto ungreased cookie sheet. Bake in 375° oven 13 to 15 minutes. Makes about 2½ doz. cookies.

Mrs. Richard Arnold

THUMBPRINT COOKIES

1 c. white sugar
1 c. brown sugar
1¼ c. margarine
3 eggs
¼ c. warm water
2 t. vanilla
4 c. flour (sifted once)
1 t. salt
1 t. soda
1 t. baking powder
1 t. cinnamon
1 c. nutmeats (optional)
1 c. chopped dates (optional)

Cream sugars and margarine. Add eggs and vanilla and beat well. Add sifted dry ingredients (and dates and nutmeats if desired). Add the warm water. Drop by tablespoons, flatten, make thumbprint in center of each cookie. Fill indentations with orange marmalade or strawberry preserves. Bake 12 minutes at 375°. Makes 42 3-inch cookies.

Mary Selden

LITTLE THINGS

A smile, a touch, a clasp of hands,
A tender word or two,
Can coax the sunshine from the clouds
And turn the skies to blue.

It's not great gifts of wealth and fame,
That make our lives worthwhile,
But all the little kindnesses
That bring the biggest smile.

Jane Meier

ALMOND BUTTER BALLS

1 c. butter
3 T. powdered sugar
1 t. vanilla
2 c. flour
1 c. chopped almonds

Cream butter and sugar. Add vanilla. Stir in flour and almonds. Blend and shape into balls. Bake in 350° oven 20 minutes. Roll in powdered sugar while hot.

Mrs. William Kremenak

OLD-FASHIONED OATMEAL COOKIES

1 c. shortening
2 c. oatmeal
1½ c. sugar
2 eggs, slightly beaten
7 T. milk
2¼ c. flour
½ t. baking powder
½ t. salt
2 t. cinnamon
½ c. raisins
½ c. nutmeats

Put shortening and oatmeal in a pan and heat slowly, stirring often because it will scorch easily if heat is too high. Cream sugar, eggs and milk (put 1 level T. soda in milk). Sift dry ingredients. Add to creamed mixture, alternately with milk and soda. Then add raisins and nuts. Lastly, add oatmeal mixture. Mix well. Drop by teaspoonsful on greased cookie sheet. Bake about 10 to 12 minutes in a 350° oven.

Edna Wagner

GUMDROP COOKIES

1 c. butter
1 c. white sugar
1 c. brown sugar
2 eggs, beaten
2 c. oatmeal
2½ c. flour
1 t. soda
1 c. coconut
1 c. gumdrops, cut fine
2 t. baking powder
1 t. vanilla

Cream butter and sugars, add eggs and blend well. Add dry ingredients and mix until smooth. Add coconut, oatmeal, gumdrops and vanilla last. Drop by spoonsful on cookie sheet and bake in a 400° oven until lightly browned. These cookies freeze well.

Mrs. Ilo Johnson

MOLASSES COOKIES

"The following cookie recipe is at least 100 years old, yet it can be made today by using these measurements. The cookies are crisp when first made, but they will become soft and mellow if stored in airtight containers. My grandmother stored them in lard cans. She always said the recipe made a 'bushel of cookies.' The unbaked dough may even be covered and kept several days."

    2 lb. brown sugar
    1 qt. molasses
    1 pt. lard
    4 t. ginger
    4 t. cinnamon
    1 t. cloves
    2 t. salt
    2 t. soda
    ½ pt. boiling water
    Flour

Mix all ingredients, adding flour last. Make a stiff dough, using about 4 lb. flour. Roll out very thin, cut and bake on a greased pan in 350° oven 8 minutes. Cool and store.

Mercedes Mills Petry

REFRIGERATOR COOKIES

    1 c. brown sugar, packed in cup
    ½ c. butter
    1 egg
    ½ t. cream of tartar
    ½ t. soda
    ¼ t. salt
    ½ c. nuts
    1 t. vanilla

Mix all together, form into roll, wrap in waxed paper and store in refrigerator. Bake as needed in 350° oven approximately 10 minutes. Slice as desired.

Mary Olson

GRANDMA'S COOKIES

    1 c. shortening
    1 c. brown sugar
    1 c. white sugar
    2 eggs, well beaten
    ¼ c. milk
    1 t. vanilla
    3 c. flour
    1 t. nutmeg
    1 t. soda
    1 t. salt

Mix sugars, shortening; add eggs, milk and vanilla. Stir in dry ingredients. Chill dough for 2 hours. Roll into balls and press with fork. Then sprinkle on sugar. Bake at 350° for 12 minutes.

Mrs. C. D. Milazzo

To separate the yolk from the white of an egg easily, break the egg into a funnel over a glass. The white will pass through and the yolk will stay in the funnel.

CORNFLAKE NOUGAT BARS

    3 T. butter
    4 c. cornflakes
    ½ c. moist shredded coconut
    4 oz. sweet or semisweet chocolate, melted
    ½ lb. marshmallows
    ½ c. coarsely chopped nuts
    ½ t. salt

Melt butter and marshmallows over hot water, stirring constantly. Remove from heat. Fold in cereal, nuts, coconut and salt. Turn out into buttered 8 x 9-inch square pans. Pat mixture evenly in pan with buttered back of spoon. Pour chocolate over top. Spread in a thin layer. Chill about 1 hour or until set. Cut into 2 x 1-inch bars. Makes 32 bars.

Sister M. Mercedes, S.C.C.

AUTUMN TREASURES

½ lb. margarine
2 c. flour
2 T. sour cream or 1 egg
2 T. sugar

Mix above ingredients together. Knead until dough is soft. Divide dough into two parts and roll out one part. Line this dough in the bottom of a 13 x 8 x 2-inch pan. Save second half for top.

Filling

2 c. sugar
6 egg yolks
½ lb. shelled, finely ground walnuts
  Grated rind of 1 lemon
6 egg whites, beaten until dry

Mix sugar and egg yolks until creamy. Add walnuts, lemon rind and egg whites. Mix well and place over pastry in pan. Roll out remaining dough and place on top. Bake at 425° until brown. When cool, sprinkle with powdered sugar and cut into squares.

Marcella Borkowski

GINGERSNAPS

Cream 1 c. shortening with 1 c. granulated sugar. Add 2 beaten eggs and 1 c. molasses. Sift 4 c. flour with 1 T. soda and 1 T. ginger. Add to above. Mix well and roll in marble-sized balls. Place on greased baking sheets and bake in 350° oven 10 to 15 minutes. Makes 4 doz. gingersnaps.

Emma Dredla

POPCORN MACAROONS

1 c. popped corn
1 c. nutmeats
3 egg whites
1½ c. powdered sugar

Run popped corn and nutmeats through a food chopper. Beat egg whites until stiff. Beat in sugar. Fold in ground nuts and popped corn and drop from teaspoon to well-greased tins. Bake 15 to 20 minutes in 350° oven.

Bernice Peers

KIRMES
(An Old-World Lebkuchen)

2¼ c. flour
½ t. baking powder
½ t. cinnamon
¼ t. cloves
¼ t. nutmeg
¼ t. salt
½ c. finely chopped candied fruit
  and peel mix
½ c. finely ground almonds
½ c. finely ground hazelnuts
2 large eggs
½ c. sugar
1 c. honey
½ c. milk

Sift the first 6 ingredients. Add next 3 ingredients. Beat the eggs and sugar. When consistency of thick cream beat in honey and milk. Add the flour mixture in small amounts. Beat smooth. Pour the batter in a jelly roll pan. Bake at 400° for 15 minutes. Turn out on a cooling rack and cool for 5 minutes. Glaze with 1 c. powdered sugar, 1 t. lemon juice, ¼ t. almond extract and 2 T. water. Cut the cookies in rectangular pieces, 1½ x 2½ inches or larger. Cookies may be stored in sealed containers for several months.

Minnie Klemme

7-LAYER COOKIE-BARS

In a 9 x 13-inch pan melt 1 stick margarine. Crush 1½ c. graham crackers. Add the following in layers:

1½ c. shredded coconut
1 12-oz. pkg. chocolate bits
1 6-oz. pkg. butterscotch or mint bits
1 12-oz. can condensed milk

Pour milk over all ingredients in the pan. Sprinkle 1 c. chopped pecans over milk. Bake at 350° for 30 to 35 minutes until done. Cut while hot.

Marcia Madsen Hays

PEANUT BUTTER FUDGE

2 c. white sugar
1 lb. light brown sugar
⅔ c. plain milk
1 jar peanut butter (plain or chunky)
1 7½-oz. jar marshmallow fluff
1 c. chopped walnuts

Stir until dissolved the white and brown sugars with the milk. Bring to a boil and boil for *exactly* 2 minutes. Remove from heat and add the peanut butter, marshmallow fluff and walnuts. Beat and pour into greased 13 x 9 x 2-inch pan. Cut when cool.

Mrs. A. W. Nutting

MAPLE BUTTERNUT CANDY

6 c. white sugar
4 c. maple syrup
¼ c. butter

Cook to form a soft ball when dropped into cold water. Remove from heat. Stir in 2 c. chopped or ground butternut meats. Stir until thick enough so that butternuts do not rise to the top. Pour into two 13 x 8-inch greased pans.

Mrs. Van B. Slack

HOLLY CANDY

1 stick margarine
34 large marshmallows
2 t. vanilla
1½ t. green food coloring
3 c. cornflakes
Red-hot candies

Melt margarine, marshmallows, vanilla and food coloring in heavy pan over low heat. Immediately pour melted mixture over cornflakes. Mix carefully, coating all flakes. Work quickly. Drop by teaspoonful on waxed paper. Flatten with spoon if necessary into irregular holly-leaf shapes. Quickly top each piece with 3 red-hot candies (close together near one end). Leave out uncovered overnight. Yield: 30 pieces.

Charlotte G. Bryant

OLD-FASHIONED TAFFY

2 c. white corn syrup
1 c. granulated sugar
2 T. butter
1 T. vinegar
¼ t. baking soda
1 t. vanilla

Combine first 4 ingredients and bring to a boil over medium heat. Stir constantly until the sugar dissolves. Continue cooking to the hard-boil stage or 260° on a candy thermometer. Remove pan from heat and stir in the soda and vanilla. Beat until smooth and creamy. Pour into a well-buttered pan before mixture thickens. When cool enough to handle, pull until the candy has a satiny finish and light color. Pull into long strips ¾ inch in diameter, and cut into 1-inch pieces with scissors. Wrap individually in waxed paper. If you want to add color, use a small amount of food color to make it appetizing. Pull the candy as soon as it can be handled for best results. Do not spare the butter in the pans, and grease the hands well.

Julia K. Sincak

> Brown sugar won't dry out with a piece of apple kept in the jar.

PLANTATION PRALINES

3 c. brown sugar, firmly packed
¼ t. cream of tartar
⅛ t. salt
1 c. milk
2 T. melted margarine
½ t. vanilla
½ c. pecans

Combine sugar, cream of tartar, salt and milk. Stir over low heat until sugar dissolves. Cook to soft-ball stage, then add margarine, vanilla and pecans. Beat until creamy. Drop from large spoon onto buttered surface.

Mary C. Hurt

SHIPWRECK

Butter a baking dish and add, layer by layer:

    Sliced onions
    Sliced raw potatoes
 1 lb. ground beef
 ½ c. chopped celery
 ½ c. chopped peppers (optional)
 1 can red kidney beans

Pour 1 can tomato soup over top and sprinkle with cheese (optional). Bake 2 hours at 350°

Mrs. Frank Wenner

TOP-OF-THE-STOVE PINTOS

  1   lb. bag pinto beans
 1¼ oz. pkg. dried onion soup mix
 10½ oz. can condensed tomato soup
  ½ c. brown sugar
  3 slices uncooked bacon
     Salt and pepper to taste

Cut bacon into small pieces. Soak beans overnight in cold water. Drain and add 8 c. fresh cold water. Cover and boil gently for 2 to 3 hours or until tender. Blend in rest of ingredients. Simmer over low heat about 1 hour. Makes 4 generous servings.

Jacqueline Shafer

SPUTNIKS

1 c. sugar	2 eggs
2 t. baking powder	¼ t. salt
1 t. nutmeg	1 t. vanilla
¼ t. cinnamon	6 T. butter
3 c. flour	1 c. milk

Beat all ingredients with an electric mixer. Drop from a teaspoon into deep fat fryer at 425°. They will turn themselves. Remove when golden brown. Roll in cinnamon sugar if desired.

Doc Kingsley

CHICKEN MANHATTAN FLAMBEAU

1 stick butter
1 onion, chopped
1 clove garlic, minced
4 chicken breasts, split
2 eggs, slightly beaten
1 c. flour
½ t. sage
½ t. poultry seasoning
2 Manhattan cocktails
  Salt and pepper to taste

In an electric skillet melt the butter on highest setting. Add onion and garlic, letting it brown while the chicken breasts are dipped in the slightly beaten eggs. Then dredge them in the flour. Place breasts in the sizzling butter: sprinkle with poultry seasoning, sage, and salt and pepper. Brown well on both sides, then pour the first Manhattan over them. Pop the lid on the frying pan quickly, lower heat to 200°, and continue cooking (covered) for 60 minutes or until the chicken is fork tender. When done, keep hot in a covered chafing dish or on a covered serving platter in a 275° oven. About 5 minutes before serving, mix the second Manhattan and warm it in a small pan over very low heat. Pour hot Manhattan directly over chicken breasts and set it aflame with a lighted match.

(Each Manhattan should consist of ¼ c. vermouth mixed with ¼ c. bourbon and 2 munificent dashes of bitters.)

Note: For freezer storage, prepare chicken according to directions but eliminate flambeau. Freeze in an airtight container. To serve, place thawed chicken in covered pan and heat in 325° oven for 30 minutes. Transfer hot chicken breasts to a chafing dish or serving platter and proceed with flambeau as directed.

Andrew J. Shafer

BEAN BAKE

1 c. chopped onion
1 lb. ground beef
½ lb. bacon
¾ c. brown sugar
1 T. vinegar
½ c. catsup
1 t. prepared mustard
1 28-oz. can baked beans
1 31-oz. can pork and beans
1 15-oz. can red kidney beans
1 small can lima beans (optional)

Brown first 3 ingredients. Add rest of ingredients and mix together. Bake uncovered in a 3 or 4-quart casserole for 1 hour at 325°.

Jeanne Flateau

HUSH PUPPIES

2 c. cornmeal
¼ c. flour
1 egg, beaten
2 c. milk
4 T. chopped onion
1 t. soda
1 T. baking powder
1 T. salt

Mix all ingredients together in a bowl. Take 1 heaping tablespoon at a time and roll in a ball. Drop in deep hot fat and fry until a golden brown. Serve with syrup or plain.

Doc Kingsley

DAD'S CHICKEN CASSEROLE

2 or 3 chicken breasts, thighs or legs, depending on size of casserole.

1 can new potatoes
1 can garden peas
1 large can chicken rice soup

Boil chicken until meat can be removed from the bones. In a greased casserole place in layers: thinly sliced potatoes, peas, chicken and part of the soup. Repeat layers and add the remaining soup. Bake 30 minutes in a 350° oven. Serves 6 to 8.

Alice E. Woods

CAJUN JAMBALAYA

1 lb. lean pork
2 T. butter
3 medium-sized onions, chopped
1 green pepper, chopped
2 garlic cloves, crushed
   Sprigs minced parsley
1 c. chopped ham
1 t. ground cloves
   Salt and pepper to taste
6 smoked pork sausages
1½ to 2 qt. beef stock
   (or ½ beef stock and ½ water)
1½ c. rice

Cut pork into very small pieces. In an iron skillet or heavy saucepan, place the butter. Sauté the pork with chopped onions, green pepper, garlic cloves and parsley until lightly browned. Add ham, ground cloves and the salt and pepper. Cut pork sausages into ¾-inch pieces. Add the sausage to the mixture, cooking 10 minutes over moderate heat. Add the beef stock and bring entire mixture to a boil. Stir in the rice and cook until rice is tender. Sprinkle filé over each serving.

Dan A. Hoover

BARBECUED BRISKET

3 to 5 lb. beef brisket
1 bottle liquid smoke
   Onion salt
   Garlic salt
   Celery salt

Sprinkle liquid smoke on both sides of brisket (use ¼ bottle per brisket). Sprinkle onion salt, garlic salt, and celery salt on each side and wrap in heavy foil. Set in refrigerator overnight.

Next day add salt and pepper and sprinkle with Worcestershire sauce. Wrap well so it is properly sealed. Place on a rack in a flat pan and bake 4 hours at 300°. Uncover. Pour a barbecue sauce over the brisket. Bake ½ hour more in the same temperature.

Willabelle Wiley

HACIENDA HAMBURGER

In a deep skillet over medium temperature, brown:

½ lb. hamburger in 2 T. vegetable oil.

Add and cook 5 minutes:

¾ c. chopped onion
1 c. sliced celery

Add:

1 16-oz. can tomatoes
1 5-oz. pkg. noodles, cooked
¼ lb. diced American cheese
½ c. chopped ripe olives
1½ t. salt
¼ t. pepper

Cover. Cook at a very low temperature 20 minutes, or pour into 2-quart baking dish and bake in 350° oven for 30 minutes. Makes 4 servings.

Golde Hoover

SPARERIB SQUARES

2 onions, sliced
5 lb. spareribs (meaty)
2 T. Worcestershire sauce
½ t. black pepper
1 t. salt
1 t. paprika
1 t. chili powder
½ t. red pepper
¾ c. catsup
2 T. vinegar
¾ c. water
2 T. flour

Cut spareribs in 2-inch pieces, sprinkle with salt and pepper and flour. Place in roaster and cover with onions. Pour remaining mixture of ingredients over the meat. Bake at 350° for 3 hours. Baste occasionally, turning meat twice. Remove cover for last 15 minutes.

Mrs. Charles Peters

EGGNOG PIE

1½ c. scalded milk
½ c. sugar
3 T. flour
1 T. cornstarch
¼ t. salt
3 eggs, separated
1 t. plain gelatin
1 T. cold water
1 T. butter
1 t. vanilla
½ c. evaporated milk, whipped
    Nutmeg

Combine salt, sugar, flour, cornstarch. Add milk gradually. Cook over hot water until thick and smooth. Pour hot mixture over beaten egg yolks, return to double boiler and cook 2 minutes longer. Soften gelatin in cold water, then add it to hot egg mixture, whipping hard. Add butter and cool. Fold in stiffly beaten egg whites, whipped milk and vanilla. Pour into shell, sprinkle generously with nutmeg. Chill for at least 2 hours before serving.

Piecrust

Mix 16 graham crackers (crushed) or 1¼ c. graham cracker crumbs with ¼ c. sugar and ¼ c. softened margarine. Press against sides and bottom of an 8 or 9-inch pie pan. Bake in preheated 375° oven for 8 minutes. Cool and fill with the pie filling.

Mrs. W. Milton Giddings

MAMA'S MOLASSES CAKE

1 c. sugar
1 egg
1 c. dark molasses
1 c. vegetable oil
1 c. hot water
1 t. (scant) soda
2 c. flour

Add soda to hot water. Mix all ingredients in order given. Bake in a 13 x 9 x 2-inch pan in a 350° oven for 30 to 35 minutes.

Ira Nethaway

PEANUT BUTTER BREAD

2¼ c. sifted flour
3 t. baking powder
½ t. salt
⅔ c. sugar
⅓ c. instant non-fat milk
½ c. peanut butter
2 t. grated lemon rind
1 egg
¾ c. water

Combine and sift flour, baking powder, salt, sugar and dry milk. Add peanut butter and lemon rind until mixture is like coarse cornmeal. Combine egg and water. Add all at once. Stir just enough to moisten thoroughly. Pour into greased loaf pan. Bake at 350° for 50 to 60 minutes. Cool before slicing.

Edith Pikelny

MOTHER'S COFFEE SOUFFLÉ

1½ t. instant coffee
1½ c. boiling water
½ c. milk
1 T. unflavored gelatin
⅔ c. sugar
¼ t. salt
3 egg yolks, beaten
½ t. vanilla
3 egg whites

Combine the coffee and boiling water in the top of a double boiler. Stir in milk, gelatin and ⅓ c. sugar, blending well. Beat egg yolks until light, and add rest of sugar along with salt. Pour a little of the warm coffee and gelatin combination into yolks, stirring constantly. Pour back into remaining coffee-gelatin mixture and blend thoroughly. Cook over medium boiling water until mixture coats a spoon, about 7 minutes, stirring continuously. Remove from heat and add vanilla. Whip egg whites until stiff and glossy, then fold them gently into the coffee-gelatin-yolk mixture. Pour into individual glasses and chill for at least 3 hours. Before serving, garnish with whipped cream and a cherry. Makes 6 servings.

Note: Top of soufflé will stay foamy, but lower part will become transparent.

Jacqueline Shafer

Where there is joy in sharing,
Where there is love to impart,
Never bare is the cupboard,
Never empty, the heart.

Laura Baker Haynes